2
1(

the small arms trade

a beginner's guide

D1352165

From anarchism to artificial intelligence and genetics to global terrorism, **BEGINNER'S GUIDES** equip readers with the tools to fully understand the most challenging and important issues confronting modern society.

anarchism
ruth kinna

anti-capitalism
simon tormey

artificial intelligence
blay whitby

biodiversity
john spicer

bioterror & biowarfare
malcolm dando

the brain
a. al-chalabi, m.r. turner &
r.s. delamont

criminal psychology
ray bull *et al.*

democracy
david beetham

energy
vaclav smil

evolution
burton s. guttman

evolutionary psychology
robin dunbar, louise barrett &
john lycett

genetics
a. griffiths, b. guttman,
d. suzuki & t. cullis

global terrorism
leonard weinberg

NATO
jennifer medcalf

the palestine–israeli conflict
dan cohn-sherbok & dawoud
el-alami

philosophy of mind
edward feser

postmodernism
kevin hart

quantum physics
alastair i.m. rae

religion
martin forward

FORTHCOMING:

astrobiology	extrasolar planets	the irish conflict
asylum	fair trade	mafia
beat generation	forensic science	political philosophy
bioethics	galaxies	racism
capitalism	gender and sexuality	radical philosophy
cloning	human rights	time
conspiracy theories	immigration	volcanoes

the small arms trade

a beginner's guide

rachel stohl
matt schroeder
col. dan smith (USA ret.)

the small arms trade

Published by Oneworld Publications 2007

ISBN-13:978–1–85168–476–2
ISBN-10: 1–85168–476–X

Typeset by Jayvee, Trivandrum, India
Cover design by Two Associates
Printed and bound in Great Britain by
Biddles Ltd., King's Lynn

Oneworld Publications
185 Banbury Road
Oxford OX2 7AR
England
www.oneworld-publications.com

Learn more about Oneworld. Join our mailing list to
find out about our latest titles and special offers at:

www.oneworld-publications.com/newsletter.htm

contents

introduction

It wasn't the four naked prostitutes that caught the world's attention. Nor was it the fifty-eight grams of cocaine, or the $500,000 worth of diamonds. What made the August 2000 raid on Leonid Minin's room at the Europa Hotel in Italy truly noteworthy were the 1500 documents scattered around the room. The documents transformed a run-of-the mill bust into an international event.

Mixed in with hundreds of receipts, correspondences, and faxes were end-user certificates and other documents that allegedly linked Minin to the sale of nearly 200 tons of small arms, light weapons and ammunition to former Liberian President Charles Taylor, whose seven-year insurgency has been described as 'a relentless campaign of sadistic, wanton violence unimaginable to those unfamiliar with ... [Taylor's] capacity to visit the abyss'.[1] Taylor shared the weapons with the equally brutal Revolutionary United Front of Sierra Leone, which routinely hacked the limbs off of civilians as part of a campaign of terror it waged against the people of Sierra Leone. Both Liberia and Sierra Leone were under UN arms embargoes at the time of the sales.

Minin denied the accusations, claiming the documents belonged to a business associate. But it was Italy's brokering laws, not Minin's alibi, that led to his release. In November 2002, the Italian Supreme Court determined that, because the weapon shipments he arranged never entered Italian territory, Minin had not violated Italian law and could not be tried. He is now a free man.[2]

The activities of illicit arms traffickers and their clients affect us all. From victims of gun violence in Brazil, to Sudanese refugees hounded by marauding militias, to the passengers on the next airliner targeted by missile-wielding terrorists, no one is beyond the reach of this deadly trade. Yet for those who do not personally suffer its ill-effects, the threat posed by the proliferation and misuse of small arms and light weapons is often a vague abstraction. It is the anthrax-laden letter and the specter of the 'loose nuke' that usually grab the headlines, not the intercepted shipments of smuggled AK-47 assault rifles and surface-to-air missiles.

As a result, many people are unaware of the pivotal role that these weapons play in terrorism, conflicts, armed violence and myriad other threats. The wars that ravaged Afghanistan, Sierra Leone, Liberia, the Sudan and dozens of other countries – wars in which millions of innocent men, women and children have died and millions more have been deprived of the economic opportunities enjoyed by their more peaceful neighbors – were (and still are) fought primarily with small arms. These weapons are also the tools of violence for many terrorists. Of the 175 terrorist acts documented in the US State Department's 2003 report on global terrorism, approximately half were committed with small arms and light weapons. Drug lords use them to eliminate competitors and assassinate government officials, abusive governments use them to suppress internal dissent and silence opposition, insurgents use them to bring down government aircraft and kill soldiers on patrol ... the list goes on and on.

Thanks to the tireless efforts of a small number of journalists, diplomats, activists, academics and policy officials, the world is beginning to awaken to the threat posed by the trafficking and misuse of small arms. Through their work in local communities, national governments, regional organizations and the United Nations, this group is raising awareness and establishing initiatives aimed at eradicating the small arms scourge. The post-September 11, 2001 focus on the threat of terrorism has generated additional media and government attention, particularly to the dangers posed by shoulder-fired missiles.

This book attempts to build upon this progress by tapping into what we believe is a large, latent interest in small arms proliferation and the integral role it plays in the historic events and political issues that are the mainstay of non-fiction best-seller lists: terrorism, armed conflict, covert operations, genocide, and so on. Most of the books on the small arms threat, however, are written by academics and specialists for other academics and specialists. We hope to fill this void by providing the intelligent lay reader with an engaging, accessible overview of the weapons, their proliferation, the threat they pose in the wrong hands and the strategies for curbing this scourge.

contents and structure

The foreword, by Dan Smith, gives a brief history of major developments in firearms technology, from the invention of gunpowder to the introduction of the Barrett .50-caliber sniper rifle in 1982. In his epilogue, he considers the future of the small arms threat and some possible strategies for addressing it, concluding with some thoughts on current control efforts and the need for a comprehensive program against small arms proliferation.

Chapters 1 to 4, by Rachel Stohl, cover the proliferation and misuse of small arms, the devastation they cause and the national, regional and international responses to them. Chapter 1 highlights the AK-47 assault rifle and examines its development and role in Cold War-related conflicts. Chapter 2 shines a spotlight on the small arms trade, and the shadowy world of illicit trafficking in particular. Chapter 3 takes an in-depth look at the costs and consequences of the uncontrolled proliferation and misuse of small arms, which fuel conflicts and violent crime in developing and affluent countries. Chapter 4 surveys the wide range of control strategies pursued by national governments, regional organizations, international institutions and non-governmental organizations, exploring multilateral agreements, export controls and eligibility criteria, marking and tracing requirements, arms embargoes, stockpile security and destruction, and other strategies.

In chapters 5 through 8, Matt Schroeder looks at the other end of the technological spectrum: man-portable air defense systems (MANPADS). Chapter 5 chronicles the early history of MANPADS, from the development of the American 'Redeye' and the Soviet 'Strela' in the 1960's to the tragic crash-landing of Air Rhodesia flight 825 – the first commercial airliner brought down by a shoulder-fired missile – in 1978. Chapter 6 takes an in-depth look at Cold War export practices, focusing on two case studies from the 1980s: the massive covert military aid program that helped the Afghan rebels end the Soviet occupation and the political battle between the US Congress and the Reagan administration over Stinger sales to the Middle East. Chapter 7 covers key events of the late 1980s and 1990s, including the acquisition and use of MANPADS by terrorists and insurgents. Chapter 8 profiles the world's reaction to an al Qaeda-affiliated group's attempt to shoot down an Israeli airliner as it left Mombasa airport in 2002.

A phenomenon as amorphous, fluid and dynamic as the small arms trade defies definitive conclusions, yet several observations link the chapters in this book:

- The proliferation and misuse of small arms and light weapons is one of the most pressing security threats of the twenty-first century.

The illicit trade in small arms contributes to many of today's security threats: terrorism, regional instability, drug trafficking, trans-national organized crime and failed states, among others. It is a scourge that knows no geographical or economic boundaries. Rich and poor countries alike suffer its ill-effects, counted in the lives of tens of thousands of people a year.

- The proliferation and misuse of small arms are truly vexing problems.

They are a smuggler's dream and a law-enforcer's nightmare. They are trafficked in thousands of ways, sought by nearly every type of violent criminal, and easily concealed; even the most deadly can be hidden in the back of a pick-up truck. They are plentiful, easy to operate, in steady supply and high demand. Most have legitimate uses, which preclude an outright ban. For these reasons, stemming the illicit trade and misuse of small arms is one of the biggest challenges of the twenty-first century.

• A multi-layered defense is needed.

There is no panacea for this problem. Reducing the threat posed by small arms requires simultaneous action on many fronts and by many different organizations.

terms and definitions

While most of the terms used in this book are defined in the glossary, a few require a bit more explanation. The term 'terrorism' is the most controversial and the most difficult to define. The reasons for this are manifold. As RAND analyst Bruce Hoffman has shown, the term 'terrorism' is very dynamic. In the last fifty years it has been used to refer to acts of repression by dictatorial governments against their own people, attacks on occupying powers by indigenous groups and violence directed at civilian targets by revolutionaries.[3] It is also highly politicized. Governments and opposition groups routinely abuse it, branding any group that opposes their policies as a 'terrorist organization'. Even when a working definition is agreed, the lines separating terrorists from guerrillas and other criminals are hazy. Guerrillas often engage in acts that many would label as terrorism and terrorist organizations often engage in criminal activities to raise funds, acquire supplies and set the stage for attacks.

With these caveats in mind, we offer the definition of terrorism given by Alex Schmid and Albert Jongman in their seminal book, *Political Terrorism*:

> Terrorism is an anxiety-inspiring method of repeated violent action, employed by (semi-)clandestine individual, group, or state

actors, for idiosyncratic, criminal, or political reasons, whereby – in contrast to assassination – the direct targets of violence are not the main targets. The immediate human victims of violence are generally chosen randomly (targets of opportunity) or selectively (representative or symbolic targets) from a target population, and serve as message generators. Threat- and violence-based communication processes between terrorist (organization), (imperiled) victims, and main targets are used to manipulate the main target (audience(s)), turning it into a target of terror, a target of demands, or a target of attention, depending on whether intimidation, coercion, or propaganda is primarily sought.[4]

We use the terms 'guerrilla' and 'insurgent' interchangeably, and use Bruce Hoffman's definition: '... [a] group of armed individuals, who operate as a military unit, attack enemy military forces, and seize and hold territory (even if only ephemerally during daylight hours), while also exercising some form of sovereignty or control over a defined geographical area and its population'.[5] For convenience sake, we also use the terms 'small arms' and 'small arms and light weapons' interchangeably. We use the term 'Proliferation' to refer to the reckless or uncontrolled spread of weapons or weapons technology. It is important to note that we do not view the spread of military technology and weapons as necessarily negative; we recognize the right of states to transfer small arms and light weapons or the technology to manufacture them to authorized recipients who protect them from loss, theft and diversion, and use them in compliance with national and international law. Finally, we use the term 'control' to refer to policies or actions aimed at preventing the acquisition and/or use of small arms by terrorists, insurgents, criminals or governments who would use them in ways that violate national or international laws. It also refers to actions taken to mitigate the damage from a successful attack by these groups.

sources

This book draws on a wide array of sources, including websites, newspaper articles, books, journals, government reports, de-classified government documents and interviews with government officials and other experts. It is important to note, however, that critical data and analysis on this subject are unavailable to private researchers. Governments are, justifiably, extremely protective of information relating to weapons holdings and development programs, clandestine operations, intelligence collection and counter-terrorism activities. Therefore many documents concerning these activities are either classified or otherwise off-limits to individuals without proper clearance. We do our best to note holes in the data, but the reader should keep these limits in mind.

acknowledgements

This book would not have been possible without the assistance of numerous colleagues, friends and family. We thank in particular Les AuCoin, Admiral Steven Baker (USN Ret.), Cate Buchanan, Herb Calhoun, Mohamed Lamine Coulibaly, Ken Epps, Tamar Gabelnick, Scott Gourley, Larry Kahaner, Lora Lumpe, Ivan Oelrich, Luke Pyles, Marv Schaffer, Robert Sherman, James Shilling and Joe Smaldone for reviewing text, offering constructive criticism, providing substantive contributions and tendering wise counsel. Joshua Kucera provided valuable references and Daniel Schaeffer, Carolyn Murphy and John Mooney provided many hours of invaluable research assistance. Rhea Myerscough contributed immensely by serving as a sympathetic sounding board and through her skilful research assistance, careful and patient editing and clear drafting of the glossary. This book also benefited from the expertise of staff of the National Security Archive and the significant contribution of dozens of government officials and other experts. We also thank our home institutions – the Federation of American Scientists, the Friends Committee on National Legislation and the Center for Defense Information at the World Security Institute – for their support and flexibility. We also appreciate the efforts of Ann Grand and the staff at Oneworld, particularly Marsha Filion. While all of these individuals contributed enormously to this book, we are solely responsible for its content and any mistakes therein.

Lastly, no large undertaking can be pursued without the love and support of family, who patiently listen to obscure anecdotes with interest and work behind the scenes to allow us these pursuits. We therefore thank and acknowledge our families, Shahna Goonerante, Quentin and Sophia Baird and Judith Smith for their unsung contribution to this project and to our lives.

Matt Schroeder
Dan Smith
Rachel Stohl
April 2006

prologue

There will one day spring from the brain of science a machine
   or force
so fearful in its potentialities, so absolutely terrifying, that even
   man,
the fighter, who will dare torture and death in order to inflict
   torture
and death, will be appalled and so abandon war forever.

Thomas A. Edison

The first human who hurled an insult instead of a stone was the
founder of civilization.

Sigmund Freud

how it might have 'be-gun'

Prehistory wasn't a fairy tale: somewhere in 'once upon a time',
hunter-gatherers learned that the stones they hurled to stun or kill
animals and fish for food could also kill other hunter-gatherers.
And, just as a group hunting together could bring down larger
prey, co-operation multiplied the chances of successfully defend-
ing territory, women, children, food stocks and other wealth.
Natural progression led to the realization that what worked for
defense could also be offensive. By the fourth millennium BCE,

when 'once upon a time' was captured in the earliest chronicles, war was a mature endeavor.

For the most part, in numerous civilizations, weapons evolved at a relatively steady pace, based on the availability of raw materials and the development of technological processes but, nonetheless, improvements – from spear to javelin, club to mace, sharpened stone to knife blade – and innovations – the bow and arrow – were confined to more efficient ways to convert muscular energy to mechanical energy, through hurling, thrusting or tensing. The discovery of the processes by which matter could be converted from one form to another by the release of chemical energy irrevocably altered the rules and the nature of warfare. Sometime between 600 and 900 CE, Chinese alchemists discovered that a mixture of sulfur, potassium nitrate, arsenic disulphide and honey would ignite when heated. They had, inadvertently, stumbled on gunpowder. Their problem was how to control the explosive forces, for the unpredictable timing and direction of the explosion often inflicted grave injuries and structural damage.

Possibly because of this unpredictability, the early uses of gunpowder were for novelties, such as enhancing the noise of exploding bamboo firecrackers. Not until the twelfth century, during the early Crusades, did European warriors come into contact with gunpowder and realize that the explosions, if confined and directed, could propel objects to maim and kill.

Making the gunpowder was the easy part: the hard part was finding a substance for the containment vessel which would hold together long enough for the force of the explosion to be directed through its mouth. The earliest cannons were either cast, from molten metal (such as bronze, iron or copper), or forged from wrought iron. Strips of iron were laid to cover a wooden core and red-hot metal rings placed around them and allowed to cool, binding the metal strips tightly together. Then the whole piece was fired in a furnace to burn out the wood core and fuse the iron strips.

going big, going small

The biggest design problem for cannon-makers was range. The larger the gunpowder charge, the further the range but physics, and the inadequacies of metal casting, limited the size of the charge. Nonetheless, according to John Barbour's poetic account of Edward III of England's campaign against Robert the Bruce's Scots, the English had a useable field artillery piece as early as 1327. The English used four cannon at the Battle of Crécy in 1346, even though their 'round shot' (or cannon balls) had little direct effect – historians credit the sound and fury of the explosions with more significance. Indeed, until men and animals became used to the mayhem that gunpowder introduced to battle, the invention was truly the terror weapon of the fourteenth century.

Over the next hundred years, cannon gradually shrank, until just two men could move some but it was not until 1430, when Florence was besieging its rival Tuscan city-state, Lucca, that personal firearms appeared. Their main use was probably simple harassment, for Lucca was well fortified and held out against the Florentine siege.

Sketches of early firearms show they were simply highly miniaturized cannons; little more than tubes into which the shooter poured black powder and pellets and discharged by applying a burning wick to a touch-hole in the tube. Simple as they may sound, they had the essential elements of all firearms: load propellant, wadding and shot, aim and fire. One very important early improvement was a wooden stock. This elevated the barrel and allowed the firer to sight directly along the barrel at the target – although the inaccuracy of early firearms made careful aiming a waste of effort.

By the mid- to late-fifteenth century, European armies were replacing traditional infantry weapons, such as pikes, with the long-barreled, smooth-bored *arquebus*. Usually less than five feet long, it employed a serpentine (S-shaped) 'matchlock' or 'fixed match' (a smoldering wick made of hemp or cotton). Moving the bottom of the 'S' brought the upper end to a touch hole bored in the right rear side of the barrel. Its military value first became apparent in 1525 in Pavia, Italy when the army of the Holy Roman Emperor, including three thousand men armed with arquebuses, supported by fifteen hundred crossbow archers, pikemen and cannon, decisively defeated the French, capturing their king and killing nearly eight thousand French men-at-arms. By the beginning of the sixteenth century, the musket was replacing the arquebus. Muskets use a spring trigger to move the match to a small pan containing a little gunpowder. The match ignites this primer, which ignites the main powder charge in the barrel.

Deliberately igniting an open pan of gunpowder near the face sounds more hazardous to the shooter than to the target but this is not the only danger. There is also the Newtonian factor: for every action there is an equal and opposite reaction or force — in firearms, *recoil*. Arquebuses and early muskets seem to have been braced on the chest, potentially highly dangerous for the shooter's breastbone and a practice that limited the size of weapons because of the force of recoil. However, by the mid-sixteenth century, firearms were almost always braced against the shooter's shoulder, which could absorb more recoil and thus allowed the development of more powerful weapons. One such weapon was the Spanish heavy musket.

A typical sixteenth-century firearm weighed about five kilograms (a .60 caliber weapon, capable of propelling a 10g lead ball). To extend the range, the Spanish developed a heavy musket that weighed eight to nine kilograms and fired an .80 to .90 caliber, 50g ball. This projectile, traveling at about three hundred meters a second, could pierce armor at one hundred meters and bring down an unarmored man or horse at five hundred. However, the weight of this weapon worked against it; it required a brace, either a forked stick or a bipod, to carry the weight of the weapon and ground the recoil, which was cumbersome. Since few men could withstand the recoil force for even one shot, the lighter matchlock musket, whose power and reliability were superior to the arquebus, proved more popular in most of Europe, remaining in use until the end of the seventeenth century.

Strangely, the design of personal firearms remained relatively static until the nineteenth century. This was not for lack of effort or imagination: King Henry VIII of England owned a unique, hand-made, short-barreled breech-loading firearm. But generally, ignorance of the characteristics of materials and inadequacies associated with manufacturing processes were major deficiencies. The one significant improvement during this period was the introduction of the wheel lock, a spring-operated mechanism which spun a roughed metal wheel against a piece of flint, creating sparks and igniting the powder in the pan. However, wheel locks were about twice the price of matchlocks, so armies largely still used matchlocks. Only when the simpler flintlock (in which sparks were generated when a piece of flint struck a metal lever that also served as a protective cap over the flash pan) appeared, around 1610, was the matchlock abandoned.

By modern standards, loading powder, wadding and ball down the muzzle, compacting them, aiming and discharging were inefficient. Well disciplined, well trained soldiers could fire three, possibly four, shots per minute. Misfires, especially before 'caps' for the flash-pan were introduced, often occurred because of dampness, the match going out or burning too low to ignite the primer or insufficient primer. Moreover, since the overall length of the musket required a soldier to stand to reload, thus exposing his entire body to the advancing lines of bayonet-wielding enemies, battles could turn on how well and how many kept their nerve in the face of cold steel.

spinning the ball: rifling and other advances

Soot from the powder and débris from the paper cartridges could easily foul musket barrels, so the spherical bullets used were made slightly smaller than the diameter of the barrel. This allowed musketeers to drop, rather than force, the ball down the barrel, making re-loading quicker. The trade-off was accuracy, because the trajectory of the bullet – having bounced down the barrel after the powder exploded – was unpredictable. Another consequence of the loose fit was 'windage' or 'blow-by' – where gases ran ahead of the bullet as it moved down the barrel. Windage lessens the effective power of the explosion, reduces the distance the bullet travels and lessens the penetration force – decreasing the deadliness of the shot.

We do not know exactly why small arms and cannon began to be rifled (have grooves cut along the inside of the barrel). One theory is that the grooves collected unexpelled powder, which otherwise might foul the barrel. Another draws a parallel to archery: by carefully arranging the angle of feathers running along the arrow shaft, the archer can make the arrow spin as it flies. The spin stabilizes the arrow and extends its range. The launcher (bow) used by the archer is an unenclosed system, which means the only part of the system that can be modified is the arrow itself. The launch systems of firearms are, for the most part, enclosed, so both the missile and its launcher can be modified to impart rotation and stabilize the shot. Both avenues were pursued. Rifled or grooved barrels were used in the mid-fifteenth century and were not uncommon in the English Civil War in the late 1640s. By the American Revolution, more than a century later, the colonists could field units of skilled sharp-shooters – often to devastating effect. The colonials formed fourteen units of riflemen, the most famous of which were Daniel Morgan's Rifles. In contrast, the British forces had just one sharp-shooting unit.

In 1807, the Reverend Alexander John Forsyth of Aberdeen, Scotland, an avid sportsman and hunter, registered a patent for a mix of chemicals (fulminate of mercury) that was so sensitive it would explode when struck with a sharp blow. Seven years later, with the invention of the metallic (first steel, then copper) percussion cap (or cup), this produced a firing system immune to most damp weather and high winds. Despite the percussion (or, as it is called in mining and construction, detonating) cap's advantages, it was not used in British military long-barrel weapons until 1842. In the twentieth century, the percussion cap was to be a key component for what became one of terror's favorite weapons – the rocket-propelled grenade.

The other major development, which perhaps really brought about the demise of the smoothbore musket, was the invention of the conical-shaped, soft, lead, 'Minie ball'. First thought of by a British officer in 1832, a reliable design did not appear until 1849. The French army Captain Claude-Etienne Minie's design was not a lead ball but a cylindrical-conical, hollow-based and grooved bullet, smaller that the diameter of the rifled barrel, making it extremely easy to load. When tapped down, the hollow base of the bullet filled with gunpowder and when the rifle was fired, the hot gas produced by igniting the powder caused the base of the shell to expand and lock into the grooves in the barrel, producing a stabilizing spin and preventing windage. The result, demonstrated in the Crimean War (1854–1858), was a more accurate, more lethal and more powerful projectile. How much more lethal? An article in the December 10, 1853 edition of *Chamber's Edinburgh Journal* claimed that the combination of the Minie ball and a new French rifle enabled a rifleman to hit a mark at 1,100 yards with nearly the same precision as a musket at 300 yards. According to the same article, Captain Minie could hit a man at 1,420 yards, three-quarters of a mile, in three out of five shots.

A further development was the expandable metallic cartridge, comprising bullet, gunpowder and explosive chemical primer in one metal case. When this was hit from the rear by the firing pin, it expanded to seal the rifle bore, except in the direction in which the rifle was pointing. However, it was not until 1970 that machine tools became good enough to manufacture the sliding bolts on rifles to such precision that they could make a seal as tight as that created by a cartridge case. This opened the way for caseless ammunition.

the american civil war: putting it all together

The American Civil War was the proving ground for technological advances in small arms, most notably the introduction and mass production of the rifled bore and breech-loaded weapons (which could be reloaded without the firer standing up). However, the dominant infantry weapon remained the .58 caliber rifled musket. In 1856, the army tested smoothbore against rifled muskets; the percentage of rifle shots hitting the target, particularly at four hundred yards, was consistently higher.

Target Distance (yards)	Smoothbore Shots Hitting Target (%)	Rifle Shots Hitting Target (%)
100	74.5	94.5
200	42.5	80
300	16	55
400	4.5	52.5

Until reliable repeaters came along, whose ammunition, pre-loaded in cases, clips, magazines or belts, was fed into the firing chamber by pulling the trigger, weapons had to be reloaded after each shot. This took nine steps for muzzle-loaders and five for breech-loaders. (Even so, this was a great advance over the sixty-seven maneuvers of the weapons drill for eighteenth-century muzzle-loaders, the forty-four for matchlocks, and the twenty-six for flintlocks.)

As mentioned earlier, Henry VIII of England is known to have owned a breech-loading gun but these weapons were not made in large numbers until the nineteenth century. Between 1836 and 1873, more than five hundred patents were issued for breech-loading long rifles: perhaps the best known was the 1863 Sharps Carbine, developed by Christian Sharps. Another was the *Henry*, a breech-loader and repeater, named after its inventor, Benjamin Henry. However, because of senior officers' fears that soldiers would waste ammunition with repeaters, the Union Army bought fewer than 1,750 Henry rifles. By the mid-nineteenth century, government arsenals, such as the one at Springfield, Massachusetts, were gearing up for mass-production. In 1855, the Army Ordnance Board recommended the rifled musket as the standard infantry weapon. The Secretary of War accepted the recommendation, something he may have rued less than a decade later when Confederate Army soldiers faced their Union Army counterparts. That Secretary of War was Jefferson

Davis, who became president of the Confederate States of America.

Of course, simply designating one weapon as 'standard' did not mean that every soldier would necessarily be issued that type of weapon. In addition to the 47,115 Model 1855 rifled muskets turned out between 1857–1861 for the Union Army, a number of smoothbore muskets were reworked by adding sights and rifling barrels to produce the Model 1863 rifled musket. Union forces also owned nearly 40,000 copies of the 1817 Flintlock (or Common) Rifle and another 70,796 copies of the Model 181 Percussion Rifle. The latter was nicknamed the 'Mississippi Rifle' as it was used to deadly effect in the Mexican-American War by that state's volunteer regiment.[1]

Having solved the range and accuracy challenges, inventors turned to the third challenge: repeat firing without reloading. One solution was to mount multiple rotating barrels around a central core. The first record of a working multi-barrel weapon is in 1718, in England, when James Puckle designed a tripod-mounted revolver-like firearm with rotating barrels. The main drawback to his design was that the multi-barrel cylinder had to be turned by hand. Even so, it could fire sixty-three shots in seven minutes – compared to twenty-one to twenty-eight for a musket. Each barrel would be charged before an encounter, allowing the firer to run off six or seven shots in quick succession. However, when the first set of shots was exhausted, the firer either had to withdraw and reload each barrel or switch weapons. There was also a problem with simultaneous discharge, caused by the hot gases from one chamber leaking into the next and prematurely igniting the powder – precluding aiming, wasting powder and bullets and being very nerve-wracking. One multi-barreled design, the Billinghurst-Requa, employed just one percussion cap and relied on a chain reaction from the first shot to ignite the other twenty-three barrels.

In 1860, Christopher Spencer offered an alternative to multiple barrels: a quickly-removable (and therefore quickly-replaceable) seven-round integral cartridge magazine – the first of its kind, which was incorporated into the Spencer Repeating Rifles used by

Union troops during the Civil War. However, some generals – particularly cavalry officers – did not like this solution, because of the weight of the extra cartridges and the magazine. They also, as noted above, didn't like repeaters because the troops used ammunition more quickly. Cavalry troops used carbines – single shot, breech-loaded, short, rifled weapons – as much to conserve ammunition as to avoid wrestling with the longer, heavier muskets.

Oblivious to the increased volume of fire on the post-Napoleonic battlefield, some Civil War generals initially employed the close-order formations of that earlier era – with lethal results for foot soldiers. Because of its industrial and demographic disadvantages, the Confederacy needed a short war if it was to survive as a new country. It took the offensive for the first two years, though without making the key tactical adjustments warranted by the new small arms – as shown at Gettysburg, when three thousand of the original twelve thousand Confederate soldiers who participated in what came to be known as 'Pickett's Charge' died while crossing open terrain. Confederate battle casualties between April 1861 and July 1863, totaled 175,000, more than were in the army in 1861. More telling is the percentage of casualties caused by small arms. Until the American Civil War, fifty per cent of battle casualties were commonly attributed to artillery fire. In contrast, Civil War battle records show that fully seventy-five per cent were inflicted by rifle bullets.

This was just the beginning. Because the Spencer was manually operated – that is, the firer opened and closed a lever or bolt, which fed a bullet from the magazine into the rifle chamber – it could fire only one bullet with each trigger pull. This meant that the rate of fire depended on the reflexes of the shooter. The quest for higher rates of fire came down to replacing the limited human with a seemingly unlimited, technological solution. Well before the end of the nineteenth century, 'automatic' firing capability existed in the Maxim and Gatling machine-guns.

The Gatling gun was named for its inventor, Richard Gatling. Developed in 1861, the original model consisted of six barrels on a rotating frame (later models had ten barrels). However, Gatling guns still had to be cranked by hand. Another American, Hiram Maxim, invented the single-barrel automatic machine-gun, which harnessed the recoil force to eject the cartridge case of the fired bullet and insert a new round into the firing chamber. Tests by the British Army in the 1880s showed rates of fire of five to six hundred rounds per minute. Ten years later, Utah gunsmith John Browning produced the Browning .30 caliber machine-gun, adopted by the US Army.

Early machine-guns had two significant problems: over-heating and weight. Overheating could be avoided either by firing in short bursts of three to five rounds (impractical on the battlefield) or by cooling the gun with water, oil or air. Oil or water added weight, while air had to be supplemented by a quick-change barrel. By the start of World War I, all the major powers had heavy (both in weight and the size – four to six men – of the gun crew) and light machine-guns. The US Expeditionary Army's Browning Automatic Rifle (BAR) was light enough, even with a twenty-round magazine, to be carried and used by one person.

Generals of both sides in World War I failed to recognize just how lethal machine-guns and the latest rifles – the German Mauser, the British Lee-Enfield and the American 1903 Springfield – had made battlefields. (One famed casualty of machine-gun fire appears to have been the German air ace, Manfred von Richthofen, 'The Red Baron', brought down by an Australian gunnery sergeant, Cedric Popkin.) Certainly the French did not. The rallying cry of the French generals was '*L'audace, l'audace, toujours l'audace*' (Audacity, audacity, always audacity). The echo from two out of seven French soldiers was silence – dead silence. By 1917, the number of French soldiers killed equaled the number that had been mobilized when the war began in 1914. Only the Americans seem to have absorbed the lessons both of their own Civil War and the first three years of World War I.

lighter and shorter

I have already mentioned the recurring concern about the increase in weight of a firearm due to the ammunition and its casing, but neither is independent of the other. As ammunition became smaller and lighter, more efficient rifles produced higher bullet velocities which forced a change from soft to hard lead and eventually to a full metallic jacket cartridge. In the late 1800s, the automatic sub-machine-gun combined rapid-fire with a stocked pistol grip and pistol-sized (sub-caliber) ammunition. Again, the emphasis was on volume, not range. In late World War I, the warring militaries began large-scale production but the weapon had little impact on the war's final outcome.

World War I convinced armies around the world that most future infantry engagements would be at 300 to 350 yard range, so long (600–800 yards) ranges were no longer a prime concern. Attention therefore shifted to combining small size and low weight with rapid-fire.

Size and weight adjustments to standard military rifles and carbines were pushed forward by the need for a compact rifle for the new paratroopers conceived in the inter-war years. The standard 1934 US Garand M-1 rifle, though an excellent weapon, was too long, heavy and unwieldy in cramped gliders and planes. Even sub-machine-guns, which in the inter-war years had become part of American folklore as the weapon of choice for criminal syndicates, found a home in commando units as World War II loomed.

a short diversion: short-barreled arms

In acknowledgement of its place in American folklore, there's room for a quick look at developments in military pistol technology before I turn to the post-World War II evolution of long-barreled weapons.

Although, during the nineteenth century, the focus was on advances in long-barreled firearms, some gunsmiths worked to improve the performance of short-barreled, single-shot weapons. One, the Connecticut native Samuel Colt, obtained British (1835) and American (1836) patents for a revolutionary revolving, multi-chambered handgun. Colt's invention had a single, non-rotating barrel, intersected by a revolving six-chamber cylinder containing the bullets, powder and percussion cap. At each trigger pull, one cap was struck and the bullet in that chamber discharged, after which the cylinder rotated to line up the next chamber with the barrel. Like rifle manufacturers, Colt's process was precise enough to make his revolver's parts interchangeable, popular in an age when most pistols were hand-made. The resistance of military leaders to the new design was stiff, partly because of the 'not-invented-here' attitude of ordnance chiefs. In 1842, Colt's first business failed, to be revived by a US Army contract during the Mexican-American War. Although Colt died in 1862, his company supplied revolvers to the Union Army during the Civil War.

The American Civil War demonstrated the difficulties of trying rapidly to reload long-barreled weapons. Even the cavalry usually dismounted to fight, both for accuracy of fire and to maintain its volume of fire. These remained acute shortcomings for the white settlers forging westward across the North American continent and for the army cavalry units expected to safeguard the expansion. Understandably, Native Americans resisted the advancing human tide, proving, much to the dismay of the US cavalry, to be highly skilled light cavalry. Rapid, sustained, gunfire was deemed to be the only effective counter to the striking power of mounted natives.

Colt pistols were hard to conceal because of their size and weight. Not so the single shot Deringer pistol, reputed to be the weapon of choice for Mississippi riverboat gamblers and women of ill-repute. The first such pistols were used in Philadelphia, where gunsmith Henry Deringer worked, in 1807. A breech-loading Deringer was patented in 1861 and an improved model in 1872, with the latter produced for forty more years.

assault rifles: efficient small weapons of mass destruction

After World War II, the victorious Western allies were intent on demobilizing and, in Europe, rebuilding. The post-war drive in the US was the re-conversion of the soldier to civilian and of industry from war machine to consumer dreams. In the Soviet Union, the Kremlin had its own version of 'never again'. Not only was Stalin intent on acquiring atomic weapons, he was determined to keep a buffer between Mother Russia and the West – and maintained a large Red Army to preserve it.

Stalin's dream coincided with Sergeant Mikhail Kalashnikov's. During the war, this self-taught engineer had built a sub-machine-gun able to fire the new 7.62mm ammunition; something senior Communist Party officials had been looking for. With official backing, in 1944 he designed a self-loading carbine, more compact, light, rugged, reliable, faster firing and easily maintained than anything Soviet troops then used: the *Avtomat Kalashnikova* (Kalashnikov Machine-gun).

It took nine years for the AK-47 to become fully operational – just in time for it to be used by the Soviet units that crushed the Hungarian Revolution. There has been a series of new models, including the AKM in 1959, the AK74 in 1974 and the RPK and PK series – but whatever the model, the enduring designation is *AK-47*.

A quarter of a century later and in a very different world, the armed forces of the Russian Federation fielded another AK assault rifle. The AK-107/108, based on a 1970s light assault rifle, the AL-7 *Avtomat Lehkiy*, designed by Yuriy Alexandrov, mimics its predecessors in its emphasis on increased accuracy and simplicity. In recognition of Alexandrov's contribution but mindful of the mesmerizing power of the Kalashnikov name, the Russians call their latest assault rifle the Alexandrov/Kalashnikov, which conveniently abbreviates to AK. It uses a simple mechanism that almost neutralizes recoil, thus giving soldiers greater control, eliminating the propensity for the muzzle to rise after each shot and cutting the re-aim and re-firing time.

Near-zero recoil was only one enhancement, as the following table shows.

Key performance characteristics	AK-47	AK107/108
Muzzle velocity	710m/sec	900-910m/sec
Rate of Fire	600 rounds/min	850-900 rounds/min
Effective Range	300 m	300 m
Weight Unloaded	4.3kg	3.6kg
Magazine capacity	30 rounds	30 rounds

In the west, the long, heavy rifles of World War II were not quickly replaced. The M14, the successor to the American M-1, designed by John Garand in 1954, did not enter service until 1957. Unfortunately, the M14 was designed for past, not future wars. In Europe, urbanization and the development of maneuver warfare meant that infantry would have fewer long-range encounters. In 1965, in the jungles of Southeast Asia, US Marines and soldiers discovered that the M14 was too large and heavy, and its ammunition too bulky, compared with the more versatile AK-47.

In the mid to late 1960s, US troops adopted the Armelite assault rifle (the AR-15, later the M16). Designed by Eugene Stoner in the 1950s, on paper the M16 compared favorably with the AK-47: it fired lighter ammunition (5.56mm), had a muzzle velocity of 975 m/sec (the M16A2 dropped to 874 m/sec) and fired 750–900 rounds/minute. However, troops in Vietnam found significant – that is to say, fatal – flaws. It was prone to fouling, because the ammunition's fine-grain powder contributed to carbon accumulation in the barrel. Until chrome-plated bores were introduced, sand, rust or other foreign bodies could cause such high friction that the first round would fail to clear the barrel.

Assault rifles were developed not so much to kill as to make the enemy seek shelter, thus suppressing their fire. However, a few specialists – the snipers – have maintained the art of long-range marksmanship. The need to disable or destroy military vehicles and other equipment at great distances with a heavy bullet led, in 1982, to the development of the US .50 caliber Barrett sniper rifle (named after its inventor, Ronnie Barrett). Although classified, its reputed effective range is just over one mile. Marine Corps snipers armed with the Barrett have struck both material and human targets. However, insurgents in Iraq have struck back; in July 2005, a six-man Marine sniper group was ambushed; all were killed and three to six sniper rifles lost.

This book is in part a narrative about two weapons – the AK-47 and man-portable air defense systems (MANPADS) – whose proliferation is so great that huge numbers are certainly in the hands of terrorist groups. But if one of the hallmarks of terror is its unexpectedness, the surprise associated with the huge stand-off distance between the snipers and their target suggests that the Barrett, and similar weapons, form their own class of 'terror' weapon.

sources

Diagram Group, 'Small arms ammunition', in *Weapons: An International Encyclopedia from 5000 B.C. to 2000 A.D.* (St. Martin's Press, 1991).

Byron Farwell, 'Mississippi Rifle', in *The Encyclopedia of Nineteenth Century Land Warfare: An Illustrated World View* (W.W. Norton and Co., 2002).

John F Guilmartin, LTC. (USAF Ret.) *Gunpowder and Galleys: Changing Technologies and Mediterranean Warfare at Sea in the Sixteenth Century* (Cambridge University Press, 1974).

David Lazenby, *The Medieval Siege Engines: Cannons* (The Middelaldercentret Project, Denmark, 1999).

Robert L. O'Connell, *Of Arms and Men* (Oxford University Press, 1989).

Randy McGuire, *St. Louis Arsenal: Armory of the West* (Arcadia Publishing, 2001).

Anthony Smith, *Machine Gun: The Story of the Men and the Weapon that Changed the Face of War* (St. Martin's Press, 2004).

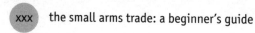

articles

Charles Q. Cutshaw, 'AK-107/108 aims for accuracy and simplicity', *Jane's International Defence Review*, July 1999.

W. M. Ferris, 'Sketch of the Progress of Invention in Offensive Arms', *The International Magazine*, January 1, 1852.

symbol of violence, war and culture

I have nothing to do with destruction that my invention carries with it. An armament in itself never kills anybody. It is the people using it who have to decide and that is where the fault lies. I will again repeat that I never made the machine-gun for people to fight with each other.

Mikhail Kalashnikov[1]

Small arms and light weapons have irrevocably shaped the landscape of modern conflict and daily life. While there is no universally accepted definition, they are generally considered to be military weapons and commercial firearms that can be operated either by an individual or a small crew. The international community most frequently uses the United Nations' definitions of *small arms*: revolvers and self-loading pistols, rifles and carbines, assault rifles, sub-machine-guns and light machine-guns; and *light weapons*: heavy machine-guns, hand-held under-barrel and mounted grenade launchers, portable anti-tank and anti-aircraft guns, recoil-less rifles, portable launchers of anti-tank and anti-aircraft missile systems and mortars of less than 100 mm caliber.[2]

Among the most widely recognized weapons in the world, the AK-47, which is part of the AK family of rifles, is a staple of modern warfare. Designed to be a reliable companion for Soviet soldiers, it has become a symbol of international resistance against colonialism and, more recently, of trans-national criminal violence, insurgency and terrorism. Although its designer, Mikhail Kalashnikov, intended it to be used to protect the Soviet Union, the AK-47 has fueled war, violence and crime across the world. The AK-47's history and its role in modern warfare make it an important starting point for a broader discussion of small arms proliferation and misuse. To this end, the following chapter examines the AK-47's cultural status, its uses during the Cold War and its legacy.

the birth of the AK-47

Mikhail Timofeevich Kalashnikov was born in 1919, shortly after the Russian Revolution, in the Siberian village of Kurya. Kalashnikov's humble beginnings gave no hint of the impact he was to have. Born into the large family of a peasant farmer, Kalashnikov and his family were exiled from their home in the Altai region to Siberia. At a young age, Kalashnikov designed items to make life easier for his family, such as a wooden mill so they could grind flour. The young inventor had only the equivalent of a high school degree when he began working for the Turkestan-Siberian railway in 1936. Two years later, he was drafted into the Soviet army where he learned to drive tanks, and, after expressing interest in firearms, was assigned to an armorer's course. Called to active duty in 1941, Kalashnikov maintained his inventive spirit as a tank driver, creating a device that counted the number of shells fired by the tank's heavy machine-gun. He also invented a tank odometer and an apparatus that allowed officers' pistols to fit through the tank's firing slots.[3]

In the battle for Bryansk, Kalashnikov's T-34 tank was hit by a shell and he was seriously wounded in the back and shoulder, wounds that would change the face of warfare. While he was in the hospital, Kalashnikov frequently talked with wounded soldiers about the need for a better military rifle and, based on these conversations, he designed his own. He has said that while he was in the hospital a soldier asked: '"Why do our soldiers have only one rifle for two or three of our men, when the Germans have automatics?" So I designed one. I was a soldier and I created a machine-gun for a soldier'.[4]

After his hospital stay, Kalashnikov worked in the Alma Alta railway depot and began experimenting with various weapon designs. They caught the eye of his supervisors, who sent them to the Ordzhonikidze Moscow Aviation Institute. Although the designs were not accepted for further development, the Institute officials recognized Kalashnikov's potential and he was rewarded with a transfer to the Institute's machine shop where working conditions were better.[5]

The price of the Soviet victory in World War II was the lives of millions of its soldiers. The death toll and their experience on the battlefield convinced the Soviets they needed to replace the SKS45 rifle, which was not well suited to the close combat they had experienced during the war. Before World War II, weapons and ammunition were designed for a range of one kilometer. The war convinced the Red Army that they needed a rifle accurate and reliable for modern warfare, which they anticipated would often be fought between soldiers spaced less than 400 meters apart. When the Soviet military announced that they were looking for a rifle to replace the SKS45, Kalashnikov submitted one of his designs to the Main Artillery Commission in Moscow. In 1946, the Commission chose his design and made several prototypes. Following field tests, one of the prototypes was accepted in 1949 as the *Automat Kalashnikova obrazets* 1947 – the AK-47.[6]

military specification: the AK-47

The Soviets hit the jackpot with their new weapon. The AK-47's superb design became the international standard for reliability and utility. Its hardiness means it can operate in all weather conditions and environments. It is cheap to produce, has a high rate of fire and is simple enough for even poorly skilled soldiers to use.

The design was not accidental: Kalashnikov did extensive research on what was essential for reliable performance, and was extremely proud of his creation:

> You see, with [designing] weapons, it is like a woman who bears children. For months she carries her baby and thinks about it. A designer does much the same thing with a prototype. I felt like a mother – always proud. It is a special feeling, as if you were awarded with a special award. I shot with it a lot. I still do now. That is why I am hard of hearing.[7]

The AK-47's bare-bones design is the secret to its success. While other assault rifles jam if only slightly fouled, the AK will fire as if it has just been cleaned, even after being dragged through the dirt. It has few components, making it easy to strip and maintain. It is gas-operated, which means its pistons are activated by the case ejection, feed and cocking mechanisms, while ammunition is fed from a banana-shaped magazine that holds thirty rounds – increasing the rotation of the bolt, which makes it more reliable. The original AK-47 uses the 7.62 × 39 mm round and can fire either single shots (for long distances) or up to 600 rounds per minute in automatic mode (for close ranges). It is extremely accurate out to 300 meters, the range within which small arms are typically used in modern wars.[8]

The weapon's success is also explained by continuous improvements, including enhancements to its stability and accuracy, moderation in the rate of fire, plastic magazines and grips, a muzzle compensator and a multi-purpose bayonet. Kalashnikov welcomed feedback from ordinary soldiers, whose lives rested on the effectiveness of his rifle. Although many models have been produced, each titled by the year of original manufacture, it is still universally known as the AK-47 or the AK. The best-known models are the AKM (modernized), a 7.62 caliber rifle which is currently the most widely used version and the AK-74 – an AKM modified to fire a 5.45 × 39 mm bullet (the M74). The AKM is also some 680g lighter than the AK-47, making it less of a burden for soldiers. Advances in manufacturing led to the mass production of the AKM model, which replaced the AK-47 in the late 1950s. As the AKM was introduced into the Soviet armed forces, the original AK-47s were given to local militias around the world. Eventually, through gun trafficking networks, these weapons made their way into the hands of terrorists, criminals and other guerrilla organizations. Today, these groups also have the more modern versions of the AK-47 in their arsenals.[9]

Kalashnikov never received any royalties, only international renown and an assortment of Soviet and Russian honors, which he cherishes: 'My aim was to create armaments to protect the borders of my motherland'. In 2003, after years of turning down offers, Kalashnikov finally signed an agreement with a German company (Marken Marketing International) that authorized the use of his name on a line of 'manly products' including snowboards, umbrellas, shaving foam, watches and penknives. He would have received thirty-three per cent of the profits from this product line but the deal never materialized. Kalashnikov now lends his name to Kalashnikov Vodka (currently sold in London) and Kalashnikov Swiss watches. He has been approached by American companies but has refused to team up with them because 'I thought if an American company used my name for profit it would have been a betrayal of the motherland'.[10]

weapons, weapons everywhere

The Soviets were delighted with the AK-47. As explained by author Larry Kahaner:

> [t]he Soviet Union had a huge conscript army of poorly trained soldiers from the various Soviet states, many of whom could not read or write and those that could often spoke different languages. This made standardized training difficult. [T]he AK suited the Soviet army because it was easy to fire, did not require a manual or training and rarely broke down.[11]

Recognizing the AK-47's exceptional utility and reliability, the Soviet Union began to distribute it through its Cold War networks, which were comprised of Warsaw Pact countries (in particular East Germany, Poland, Romania, Bulgaria and Hungary) and non-pact allies (North Korea and Yugoslavia). These countries purchased and produced millions of AK-47s: 'Politics aside, the AK-47 was the perfect item to sell. It was cheap, easy to produce in great quantities, simple to transport, good value for the price, easily repairable, and it came with a ready market'.[12]

China and Poland began production of their own versions of the AK-47 in 1956 and Hungary, Bulgaria, East Germany, North Korea and Yugoslavia followed soon after. The Soviets encouraged production and did not charge licensing fees. An estimated fifteen to twenty million of the Chinese variant, the Type 56 rifle, were produced for China's own military and for export. East Germany and Poland each produced an estimated two million; Hungary, Romania and Bulgaria together are believed to have produced an additional two million and Yugoslavia and North Korea an estimated four to five million (North Korea accounts for two-thirds of that total).[13] This list is not exhaustive, as variants of the AK-47 have been manufactured across the world.

Kalashnikov had no idea his weapon would have such world-wide appeal:

I made it to protect the motherland. And then they spread the weapon [around the world] – not because I wanted them to. Not at my choice. Then it was like a genie out of the bottle and it began to walk all on its own and in directions I did not want.[14]

The widespread production of AK series rifles contributed to their proliferation. Between seventy and a hundred million rifles are in circulation – ten times the number of Uzis or M-16s. AK-47s are in the national inventories of at least fifty-eight countries and have been used by states and non-state actors in conflicts in over ninety.[15]

the AK-47: cultural icon

The AK-47 is more than just an effective tool of war; in many countries, it is also a cultural icon. It is featured on the coats of arms of Zimbabwe and Mozambique and previously on that of Burkina Faso (until it adopted a more peace-oriented symbol), and appears on the Mozambican flag and currency. Not all Mozambicans are happy with their country's homage to its revolutionary past. In June 2005, the Mozambican parliament approved a law to change the flag and national emblem and ran a competition for a new design to reflect the country's return to peace. Some Mozambicans question the use of scarce resources on such an endeavor, but for many, removing the gun from the flag is an important symbol of their country's commitment to peace. As one Mozambican legislator put it, 'As a peaceful country, you can't have a flag with a gun on it. For children growing up now in peace, they see a flag with a gun on it and it doesn't make sense'.[16]

Non-state groups also use AK-47s and other guns in their logos. The insignias of Hamas and the An-Najah Students Cell of the Islamic Palestine Block use the M16 and three well-known terrorist groups use the AK-47 in their insignias to signify a commitment to armed struggle. The Palestinian Liberation Front, which operates in Israel, Lebanon and Egypt, has AK-47s in its emblems and the Salafist Group for Call and Combat, which operates in Algeria, Chad, Mali, Mauritania and Niger, has a sword and an AK-47 in its symbol. Hezbollah's symbol includes a fist clutching an AK-47, with the AK forming the 'l' of 'Allah'.[17]

In South Africa, an anti-apartheid music group named itself AK-47. The name 'Kalash' is common in some countries in Africa. When Kalashnikov was introduced to guerrilla fighters in Mozambique, they told him that they had named babies after his weapon.[18] Kalashnikov takes great pride in this:

> When I met the Mozambique minister of defense, he presented me with his country's national banner, which carries the image of a Kalashnikov sub-machine-gun. And he told me that when all the liberation soldiers went home to their villages, they named their sons 'Kalash'. I think this is an honor, not just a military success. It's a success in life when people are named after me, after Mikhail Kalashnikov.[19]

Images of the AK-47 abound in today's conflicts. Videos of Osama Bin Laden show him firing an AK-47 or sitting with one close at hand. Film of Saddam Hussein's capture by US forces shows two AKs in his hideout. Many visitors to the Ishmash company (where the AK-47 was originally produced) wear t-shirts advertising the 'AK-47 World Destruction Tour' with Chechnya, Afghanistan, the Gaza Strip, the Congo and Nagorno-Karabakh listed as tour stops.[20]

the AK-47: cold war tool

The reliability of the AK-47 explains its ubiquity in Cold War conflicts. In the Vietnam War, the North Vietnamese used the AK-47 (predominantly the Type 56 Chinese variant). Chris McNab claims that three AK-wielding Vietcong could fire ninety rounds in four seconds. The majority of American troops relied on the M14, and later the M16, which fared poorly in the jungle. According to Larry Kahaner, Vietcong forces were known to leave behind US rifles after killing American soldiers or raiding their caches, while US forces 'routinely took AK-47s from enemy dead and used them instead of their M16s. This practice became so commonplace that soldiers in the field officially were banned from using AK-47s, because their distinct sound attracted friendly fire'.[21]

Its reputation solidified by its successes in the Vietnam War, the AK-47 was frequently used in struggles in other regions. The 1970s and 1980s saw a huge influx of small arms, including AK-47s, into Central America. While the United States and the Soviet Union had a hand in these transfers, they tried to conceal their involvement, using proxy sources and dealers. The United States routinely purchased Soviet bloc weapons for insurgent groups. In fact, the CIA and US Department of Defense are believed still to maintain stocks of Soviet-bloc weapons, including AK-47s, which originated from Eastern Europe and entered the United States through Wilmington, North Carolina. When the US did not supply weapons, other allies picked up the slack. After the

United States officially cut off military assistance to Guatemala in 1977, Israel supplied the Guatemalan government with fifteen thousand Galil rifles (the Israeli variant of the AK), Uzis, M-79s, bazookas, mortars and production rights for the Galil. Similarly, when the United States stopped covert aid to the Nicaraguan Contras, the head of the Nicaraguan Democratic Force – the largest rebel group – claimed they had obtained ten thousand Polish AK-47s using $15 million from a non-US source.[22]

The Communist arms pipeline ran through Cuba, which received weapons from the Soviet Union, its Warsaw Pact allies and North Korea. Cuba then supplied weapons to other countries, for example to the Sandinistas in Nicaragua, who relied on the AK-47 as their main weapon of war and, it is believed, to pro-Communist rebels in Angola. In El Salvador, FMLN guerrillas received AK-47s to fight the US-backed government. These were provided by Honduran military officials from CIA weapons caches left over from the Nicaraguan civil war. According to Frank Smyth, who traveled with FMLN guerrillas, the AK-47s boosted the rebels' morale; they believed the weapons gave them tactical advantages – longer range and heavier bullets – over the American weapons both sides had been using.[23]

In Central America, both sides were often armed with AK-47s. As mentioned earlier, the Nicaraguan Contras were believed to have ten thousand Polish AK-47s in their arsenal, even though Polish officials ridiculed the idea that they would sell weapons that could be used against the Marxist Sandinistas. US officials believed the weapons could have been diverted, although Poland was eager to obtain cash to pay off foreign debts. The shipment was reportedly sent from the Bulgarian port of Burgas via an unidentified Latin American country hostile to the Sandinista government. AK-47s used by the Contras are also thought to have come from stocks confiscated by Israel from the Palestinian Liberation Organization, supplied to curry favor with the United States.[24]

Although most Cold War-related armed conflicts have ended, the effects of the arms used to fight them persist. In many former Cold War battlegrounds, the number of deaths and level of violence has increased since the conflicts' ends. Moreover, weapons continue to flow into the region. Although some of its wars have been over for more than a decade, significant quantities of arms still stream to Central America. Between 1996 and 1999, the US government sent $376,000 worth of small arms to Costa Rica, El Salvador, Honduras and Panama and authorized private industry sales totaled over $66 million.[25]

The availability of a wide range of guns – including handguns, rifles and machine-guns – has had a significant effect on violence and crime. Easy access has facilitated the acquisition and use of these weapons by criminals, gangs and drug traffickers. For example, ineffective disarmament, demobilization and reintegration (DDR) programs in Nicaragua, which failed to prevent the re-arming of some twenty thousand men in the mid-1990s, have contributed to armed violence and crime in that country. In 2000, forty-four per cent of crimes in Nicaragua involved military-style weapons. Other Latin American countries also suffer from high levels of gun violence. Although murder rates in El Salvador have decreased since the end of the war in 1992, the proportion of murders committed with firearms rose from fifty-five per cent in 1990–95 to seventy-five per cent in 1999. In 2001 in Honduras, firearms caused eighty-two per cent of deaths in young adults. Thirty-six per cent of the deaths involved AK-47s. In comparison, of the 582 murders reported in Canada in 2002, only a quarter were committed with firearms.[26]

spreading weapons of individual destruction

It [the AK-47] is a means of securing peace. I feel sad when I hear about its misuse.

Mikhail Kalashnikov[1]

Every year, small arms and light weapons are responsible for many hundreds of thousands of deaths in conflict, an estimated 200,000 deaths in peaceful countries and at least three times as many injuries. Their widespread availability prolongs conflicts and allows more people to participate in them. After conflicts end, small arms often remain in communities, increasing the likelihood that conflicts will re-ignite or spread. Uncontrolled weapons proliferation and misuse fuels violence and criminal activities, disrupts development assistance and interferes with efforts to deliver food, medicine and supplies. Education and healthcare are short-changed, civil structures fail to take root and economic growth is retarded, condemning millions to abject poverty or hardship.

Although his weapon has become synonymous with devastation, Kalashnikov absolves himself of responsibility for its evils:

It is not my fault that the Kalashnikov became very well-known in the world; that it was used in many troubled places. I think the

11

policies of these countries are to blame, not the designers. Man is born to protect his family, his children, his wife. But I want you to know that apart from armaments, I have written three books in which I try to educate our youth to show respect for their families, for old people, for history.[2]

Despite his intentions, Kalashnikov's rifle, and the many other weapons like it, are sold by black marketeers to criminals, terrorist and insurgents around the world. This chapter explains how small arms enter the black market and are acquired by terrorists and insurgents. It also highlights the activities of illicit arms brokers and profiles two of these shady characters.

from here to there: the small arms and light weapons trade

In 2002, the *Small Arms Survey* estimated that some 638.9 million small arms and light weapons were in circulation, including approximately 241.6 million military firearms, 22 million shoulder-fired rocket launchers and about 781,000 mortars. Approximately 378 million of that total was believed to be in civilian hands.[3]

Small arms can be purchased from a variety of suppliers, the number of which has grown since the end of the Cold War. Made obsolete by upgrades or superfluous by the Cold War's sudden end, weapons from that era are now sold – legally and illicitly – by countries seeking to raise money quickly. New small arms are also readily available: 1,200 companies in over ninety countries produce approximately eight million brand-new weapons every year. In 2002, the average black market price of a used AK-47 ranged from $3,800 in India, to $40 in Cambodia and $10 in Afghanistan. AK-47s are sometimes traded for livestock or other commodities. No matter how you price the individual weapons, the small arms trade is big business, worth an estimated $5 billion a year – $4 billion in legal sales and $1 billion in illicit sales.

What makes a sale legal or illicit? The *Small Arms Survey* defines a legal transfer as one that conforms to international law and the national law of the importing and exporting states while an illicit transfer violates those laws. Ambiguities and loopholes often make it difficult to categorize a sale as legal or illicit. For example, some sales are legal under national export law but violate international humanitarian or human rights law.[4]

Small arms and light weapons are traded on three kinds of markets: white, black and grey. As defined by the *Small Arms Survey*, white market transfers (or legal transfers) occur 'with either the active or passive involvement of governments or their authorized agents and in accordance with both national and international law'. Legal sales are conducted in accordance with UN arms embargoes and follow national regulation and practice. Black market arms deals (or illicit transfers) occur 'in clear violation of national and/or international laws and without official government consent or control; these transfers may involve corrupt government officials acting on their own for personal gain'. Black market sales are generally to individuals or criminal organizations. Grey market transfers, which often involve governments or their agents, 'exploit loopholes or circumvent national and/or international laws or policy'. Insurgent groups and embargoed governments are often the recipients of grey market transfers. The line between white and grey market sales is often blurry. For example, covert sales may be government-sponsored but nonetheless violate international law, defy UN arms embargoes or ignore national policies. The value and volume of sales on the grey market may actually be larger than on the black market.[5]

Small arms are diverted from legal to illicit markets in a variety of ways. First, small arms and light weapons enter the black market via corrupt or negligent government agents. These officials provide export licenses in exchange for bribes or fail to adequately check the documentation associated with the transfers, resulting in the delivery of weapons to countries under embargo. For example, UN investigators identified numerous violations of the arms embargoes on Angola and Liberia by the governments of both supply states and transit states (countries through which weapon shipments pass on their way to the recipient state).[6]

Second, government arsenals and stockpiles are occasionally looted during several internal crises. In Albania in 1997, national arsenals were stormed by mobs angered by a failed government pyramid scheme. More than half a million Albanian weapons flowed into the Balkans and beyond, contributing to violence in an already tense region.

Third, weapons in insecure or poorly managed civilian and government stockpiles are vulnerable to theft and loss. Every year an estimated 8,500 weapons are stolen from or lost by the South African Police and the South African Defence Force. Approximately one million small arms are stolen from, or illicitly re-sold by, private owners in Europe, Asia, Africa and the United States.[7] Fourth, weapons are sold by soldiers. For example, in 1993 more than three thousand Russian soldiers sold their personal weapons to supplement their meager and erratic wages. In Israel, military officers have sold weapons to Palestinian fighters even with the knowledge that the weapons might be used against them or their colleagues.[8]

Privately owned small arms, which constitute sixty per cent of the global supply, are a fifth significant source of illicit weaponry. In the United States, at least half a million weapons acquired during burglaries end up on the black market each year. Since this number only reflects reported thefts, the real total is likely to be much higher. Handguns form the majority of stolen US guns (sixty per cent); .38 mm revolvers are the most popular (over twenty per cent). Rifles make up twenty-two per cent and shotguns the remaining seventeen per cent. In South Africa, the Police Services conclude that 'the main internal source of illegal firearms remains the theft, robbery or loss of firearms in legal possession'. Between April 1, 2004 and March 31, 2005, approximately forty-three guns were stolen there every day, a total of 15,837 in that year.[9]

Sixth, weak national laws governing the sale, purchase and ownership of small arms allow their diversion to the black market. Some countries have no laws – or at best weak ones – regulating domestic firearms purchases or possession, which allows people to purchase dozens of weapons at a time. The unscrupulous exploit these laws, by engaging in 'straw purchasing', when someone with a clean record buys numerous weapons and resells them, usually illegally, to those who cannot buy them. These weapons often cross national borders and are resold in countries with more restrictive gun laws. For example, the United States has less restrictive gun purchasing laws than Mexico and Canada, and weapons of US origin reportedly account for approximately fifty per cent of illegal handguns in Canada and eighty per cent of the arms recovered from crimes in Mexico. The effects of these illegal purchases can be deadly. The Cardinal of Guadalajara, Jose Posadas Ocampo, was assassinated in 1993 with an American gun. A year later, the PRI presidential candidate Luis Donaldo Colosio was killed in Tijuana with a .38-caliber Taurus pistol smuggled from the United States.[10]

Finally, craft producers (unlicensed gunsmiths) make weapons to sell on the black market. Although economically, craft production is only a small part of global small arms production, these weapons support armed violence and instability. In Chile, for example, craft production fuels the activities of criminals and gangs. Similarly, the arsenals of Filipino Islamic separatist groups and organized criminal gangs are stocked with weapons and ammunition made by craft producers.[11]

Small arms are an essential component of the global trafficking of illicit goods. For example, the illegal diamond trade connects the governments of Liberia, Togo and Burkina Faso to arms brokers in Eastern Europe and Russia and diamond dealers in Belgium and Israel. Such interconnectedness has made it nearly impossible to tackle the trade in arms separately from trades in other commodities. Rebel groups, criminal syndicates and terrorist organizations utilize these networks to fund their operations. Arms are both a commodity and a medium of exchange. The Revolutionary Armed Forces of Colombia (FARC) is reported to make nearly $500 million a year in drug trade profits, which includes the value of the weapons they purchase with drugs. One expert found that 'this barter was so institutionalized that a *de facto* exchange rate of one kilo of cocaine sulfate per AK-47 was established as the going rate'.[12]

Arms dealers rely on many accomplices, such as pilots, financiers, freight forwarders and corrupt government officials, among others. These individuals often operate out of several different locations; the broker may be located in a different country from the freight forwarder, while the financier is in a third country, and the pilot and plane are registered in yet another country. In some cases, these dealers exploit legislative loopholes to comply with the letter, but not the spirit, of national laws. With an international cast of characters operating in a variety of countries, trafficking networks are often able to stay one step ahead of the law.

VICTOR BOUT

Born in 1967 in what is now Tajikistan, Victor Bout holds a degree from the Military Institute of Foreign Languages in Moscow and is believed to speak at least six languages. While other arms dealers focus on the Middle East, Europe, or Asia, Bout has conducted most of his deals in Africa, the scene of dozens of conflicts since the mid-1990s. Bout and his associates have operated in Angola, Cameroon, Central African Republic, DRC, Equatorial Guinea, Kenya, Liberia, Libya, Congo-Brazzaville, Rwanda, Sierra Leone, South Africa, Sudan, Swaziland and Uganda. The United Nations accuses him of violating the arms embargoes in Angola, Sierra Leone and Liberia. He chartered several of the thirty-seven (UN-documented) flights that ferried weapons to the Angolan rebel group UNITA between July 1997 and October 1998.[13]

Bout is particularly adept at getting around national and international arms embargoes. He uses his own organizations to complete his deals, including air charter companies (his main company is Air Cess), freight forwarders and a complex network of companies owned by partners. Bout's air operations have been based in Sharjah (in the United Arab Emirates) and he often changes the registration of his aircraft from one country to another. He is believed to have sold weapons to all sides of

VICTOR BOUT (cont.)

the majority of civil wars in Africa and was involved in arms sales to both the Taliban and the Northern Alliance in Afghanistan. He reportedly made $50 million from sales to the Taliban in the late 1990s. According to media sources citing US government officials, Bout's aircraft transported cargo in Iraq and his companies have received federal funds totaling millions of dollars from US contractors. Companies such as FedEx, Kellogg and Brown & Root (a former subsidiary of Halliburton) have reportedly used his companies to transport military and construction supplies.[14] Bout lives openly in Moscow, even though there is an Interpol warrant for his arrest.

making deals

The shady characters that facilitate illicit arms transfers are known as brokers. An arms broker is 'a private individual or company that acts as an intermediary between a supplier and a recipient of weapons to facilitate an arms transaction in return for a fee'.[15] Just as conflicts have changed since the end of the Cold War, so have the brokers. During the Cold War, brokers often worked on behalf of governments who did not want to get their hands dirty providing covert weapons to allied regimes and armed groups. When the Cold War ended, arms brokers had to adapt to a new way of business or risk being out-maneuvered by competitors. The community of arms brokers has become much more diverse. Now, instead of supplying weapons on behalf of the United States or the Soviet Union, many simply provide arms to the highest bidders, without particular loyalties. Victor Bout is known to supply arms to some of the bloodiest dictators in Africa, with no political agenda, while Sarkis Soghanalian is identified as belonging to the older breed; he sold weapons to defeat Communism and has worked closely with US covert operations.

Successful arms brokers understand the black market and how to move goods on the edge of legality.[16] They know how to take advantage of the supply routes developed during the Cold War and have strengthened the links between the trade in arms and other commodities. Some operate in the shadows, unknown to national and international law enforcement agencies, while others conduct their business in full view and are known intimately to government officials. Brokers build up clandestine transport practices and develop strong relationships with corrupt officials. As discussed further in Section 2, amateur arms brokers do not last long in this complex world.

Using complicated trafficking routes and exploiting unsynchronized national laws, arms brokers manipulate legal networks for illegal purposes. Governments often use the same networks and routes to transport grey market arms. Many brokers, such as Victor Bout, traffic weapons for governments to help finance future black market deals. This inextricable linking of legal and illegal commerce complicates the effort to stop illicit arms trafficking. As Wood and Peleman point out, 'cross-border mergers between airlines, marketing alliances, leasing, chartering, franchising and offshore registration of fleets, crews and companies, all make it even more difficult to monitor and regulate the airspace and freighting industry'.[17]

Black and grey market small arms are moved by air, ground and sea transport, just like legal commodities. Regardless of the mode of transport they use, arms brokers use fake documents, including false bills of lading and end-use certificates or incomplete manifests to ensure the safe passage of their illegal cargo. Using these documents, weapons are transported by indirect or circuitous routes and through third countries whose governments are willing to allow weapons to cross their borders. When Liberia and Sierra Leone were under a UN arms embargo, arms brokers relied on corrupt governments and officials to transfer arms. Traffickers used false end-user certificates to ship weapons from Eastern Europe to Liberia through countries such as Libya and Nigeria. Between May and August 2002, two hundred tons of guns and ammunition were shipped to Monrovia from Belgrade using false Nigerian end-user certificates.[18]

Arms brokers often disguise their wares as more innocuous items. Weapons have been smuggled into refugee camps in Zaire masquerading as humanitarian aid and into Burundi as farm implements. Co-opted by arms merchants, some aid organizations in the Sudan have served as fronts for gun-running. In Central America, arms intended for Colombian guerrillas were carried across Costa Rica hidden in shipments of vegetables. Code names may be used for clandestine transport. In one intercepted communication between Colombian guerrillas, grenades were referred to as pineapples, ammunition as food and the dollars that paid for them as lettuce.[19]

SARKIS SOGHANALIAN

One of the world's most notorious arms dealers, Sarkis Soghanalian is often referred to as 'the merchant of death'. Born in 1929 or 1930 in what is now Turkey, Soghanalian was raised in Lebanon from the age of ten. Since 1979 he has lived in the United States. He is an old-school arms dealer, who worked with the US government during the Cold War and has armed some of the world's best-known dictators, including Saddam Hussein, General Anastasio Somoza in Nicaragua and Mobutu Sese Seko of Zaire. At first, Soghanalian trafficked mostly in weapons from Eastern bloc countries but began selling US weapons in the early 1970s. More recently, he organized a transfer of 10,000 AK-47s that ended up in the hands of the Colombian rebel group FARC, although he claims it was intended for the government of Peru.[20]

Soghanalian has flaunted his relationship with the United States. In the mid-1980s he allowed a CNN reporter to accompany him to Iraq and attend his negotiations with military officials. In 1987, the deputy director of the CIA flew to Panama in Soghanalian's private jet in an attempt to get General Manuel Noriega to cede power. Soghanalian insists that he received the US government's blessing for most of his arms deals but not all

SARKIS SOGHANALIAN (*cont.*)

were officially sanctioned. For example, he has served jail sentences for fraud and for conducting arms sales to Iraq in violation of the US Arms Export Control Act, which he claims was done at the behest of the US government. Additional charges of weapons export violations and wire fraud were mysteriously dropped, including indictments for brokering a sale of machineguns to Mauritania, allegedly because of classified co-operation with US intelligence services. In addition, he helped uncover a counterfeit printing operation in Lebanon and contributed to the unsuccessful attempt to secure the release of the American hostage Terry Anderson.[21]

Arms brokers circumvent national arms controls and international arms embargoes by exploiting corrupt or negligent government officials and shortcomings in national laws. They often act with impunity, as most countries do not have laws to regulate their activities and there is often little international co-operation on their prosecution. The whereabouts of some infamous arms brokers are well known but many continue to conduct their business freely and live without fear of capture. Victor Bout is a good example: he gives interviews to *The New York Times*, contributed to the 2005 film, 'Lord of War', and is frequently seen eating at his favorite sushi restaurant in Moscow. The United Arab Emirates has refused to co-operate with US officials in identifying his UAE based companies and both the British and US military have acknowledged they inadvertently used his companies to transport cargo in Iraq.[22] When countries interrupt his operations by shutting down affiliated front companies, Bout simply moves his operations elsewhere.

However, the world in which illegal arms dealers can operate is slowly getting smaller. Some forty countries have legislation covering the activities of arms brokers and the United Nations is laying the groundwork for an international convention (see

Chapter 4).[23] Unfortunately, many existing laws are not actively enforced or do not cover citizens operating beyond their home country. With so few countries implementing brokering laws, many unscrupulous characters are still able to operate without interference.

costs and consequences

I'm proud of my invention but I'm sad that it is used by terrorists. I would prefer to have invented a machine that people could use and that would help farmers with their work – for example a lawnmower.

Mikhail Kalashnikov[1]

The effects of the proliferation and misuse of small arms vary from country to country and conflict to conflict. Some are obvious – the deaths and injuries caused by small arms speak for themselves. Others are more subtle – lost economic and social opportunities may take years to materialize. Asked how he felt about the destructive effects of his weapon, Kalashnikov said:

You see, maybe all these feelings come about because one side wants to liberate itself with arms. But in my opinion, it is the good that prevails. You may live to see the day when good prevails – it will be after I am dead. But the time will come when my weapons will be no more used or necessary.[2]

Small arms proliferation often perpetuates cultures of violence, in which weapons are seen as symbols of power, dominance and worth and as tools for resolving conflicts. The cycle of violence – when fear causes people to take up arms, which leads to violence and insecurity and causes people to arm themselves further – undermines family structures and the authority of community leaders and contributes to crime and impunity.[3]

In Afghanistan, violence and war have shaped generations. A popular Afghani saying is 'You earn your living from the muzzle of a gun'. In January 2002, the UN special representative for human rights in Afghanistan told a news conference that the 'rule of the gun' must end for Afghanistan to have any chance of true freedom.[4] This culture has made disarming ex-combatants, warlords and civilians difficult – and effective strategies remain elusive. The situation in Afghanistan is, unfortunately, not unique. This chapter will examine the economic, societal and political costs of weapons proliferation, in conflict zones and areas at peace, highlighting cultures of violence and the use of child soldiers. It will also illustrate the transformation of weapons from tools of war to instruments of lawless violence and terror.

human security impacts

Small arms misuse affects everyone – from the individual to the international community. Human rights abusers use them to commit extra-judicial executions and forced disappearances and for torture. Women and girls endure rape, violence, abductions, slavery and forced prostitution at the barrels of guns, while young men die from gun injuries in alarming numbers. Even those that are not directly targeted can be victims, suffering the psycho-social trauma associated with living through war and observing violence.

Conflicts waged with small arms force millions of people from their homes every year. In December 2005, an estimated twenty-four million people in at least fifty countries were on the move due to armed violence. Populations are often affected by small arms even when a conflict has ended, as refugees fear returning home because of small arms-wielding criminals in their communities or on their travel routes. The proliferation and misuse of small arms also affect social structures indirectly. Families are weakened and support for children is disrupted when parents are killed by small arms or when small arms violence forces children to flee alone. The introduction of firearms to a society may also undermine traditional structures based on respect for tribal elders. Empowered by guns, village youths are less likely to heed the orders of community leaders.[5]

Small arms can change established patterns of warfare and society. The Karamajong in Uganda traditionally used spears to fight rival groups and raid each others' cattle, which led to relatively few deaths. When the AK-47 became widely available, the dynamics of tribal warfare changed. Not only did the rate of deaths and injuries increase, but the AK-47s also allowed unrequited hostilities to be acted on. In other areas of East Africa, guns became a widely used medium of exchange. In 1998, for example, AK-47s were worth $200, routinely traded for three or four cattle and were even used in dowries.[6]

In post-conflict societies, small arms often hinder peacekeeping and peace-building. Afghanistan and Iraq provide many examples of the difficulty of establishing security, upholding the rule of law, and successfully transitioning to peace in small arms-infested areas. Businesses have been unable to re-open and badly needed repairs to roads and power supplies have delayed because of continued violence and instability. Educational opportunities are limited as schools remain closed because of insecurity, fear, or displacements of parents and students, and because teachers are unwilling or unable to return to schools.

In underdeveloped nations recovering from war, the proliferation and misuse of small arms limits access to food, water and livelihoods. Interference with basic supply lines and transport routes leaves markets closed, supplies scarce and fields fallow. The presence and threat of small arms affects land-use patterns, harvesting, livestock production and grazing practices and can limit investment in commercial activities.[7] Because health services may be limited during conflicts and resources may be consumed in treating injuries from firearms, weapons proliferation also contributes to suffering from preventable and treatable conditions.

Small arms proliferation and misuse also impedes humanitarian assistance. Life-saving aid is often interrupted or suspended, with dire consequences for defenseless populations. Aid workers are targets for extortion, theft and rape, prompting aid agencies to spend their resources on security for their staff rather than on much-needed assistance for vulnerable populations. In a survey of more than two thousand humanitarian and development workers in ninety countries carried out by the Centre for Humanitarian Dialogue and *Small Arms Survey*, thirty-three per cent reported that armed conflict had caused the suspension of operations or projects during the previous six months. Similarly, twenty-six per cent of the respondents reported that armed crime had caused a suspension of their activities.[8]

Small arms proliferation and misuse drain resources away from rebuilding and development, causing continued economic hardship and lack of economic opportunities. These conditions deprive needy populations of resources necessary to rebuild and pursue their livelihoods. In particular, support services and job training may be minimized.

Child soldiers, which are used by government forces, government-supported paramilitaries, or other armed groups in over twenty countries, are a tragic corollary of the proliferation of small arms. Because assault rifles and other military firearms are often light-weight and easy to use, a young child can easily be taught to fire them. Where the adult population has been decimated by years of war, children replace the men who would normally serve as soldiers. For example, during the decade-long civil war in Sierra Leone, the adult population was largely eliminated, leading to the widespread use of children in combat, which allowed the conflict to rage on for years. The phenomenon of child soldiers is not unique to Africa. The first American soldier killed in Afghanistan during Operation *Enduring Freedom* (a thirty-one year old Green Beret, Nathan Ross Chapman) was reportedly shot by an AK-wielding fourteen year-old boy.[9]

prolonging conflict

south asia: pipeline of death

Weapons left over from Cold War battles have ravaged the countries of south Asia for decades, particularly Pakistan and Afghanistan. During the 1970s and 80s, the United States and the Soviet Union sent millions of small arms and light weapons to their allies in the region. These weapons not only fueled the war in Afghanistan during the 1980s and again in 2001, they also changed the security landscape of neighboring Pakistan.

When the Soviet Union invaded Afghanistan in 1979, the Red Army was far better armed than the militias they faced, the *Mujahedeen* ('Holy Warriors' or 'strugglers'). These anti-Communist Muslim guerrillas initially obtained AK-47s by raiding Soviet arms caches. Eventually, with American assistance, they acquired large quantities of AK-47s and other, more sophisticated, weapons. With the United States fully involved behind the scenes, the *Mujahedeen* could better challenge the Soviets. As it did later in Central America, the CIA purchased hundreds of thousands of AK-47s, from China, Poland, Egypt and Turkey, which it passed on to the *Mujahedeen*. Using Soviet Bloc weapons had two main advantages: the *Mujahedeen* preferred using AKs because of their reliability and the CIA preferred supplying them because it allowed the United States to deny its involvement.

The CIA created a pipeline that channeled weapons from its sources, via Pakistan, to Afghanistan. Weapons 'usually entered Pakistan through Islamabad or Karachi. From there, arms went to staging areas in the towns of Quetta and Peshawar near the Afghan border then into Afghanistan'.[10]

The influx overwhelmed Pakistan's ability to regulate the flow of arms through its territory. During the decade-long conflict, an estimated 400,000 US-supplied AK-47s and millions of other weapons entered Pakistan. Although these guns were intended for the *Mujahedeen*, many were diverted to criminals in Pakistan, revolutionaries in Iran and other actors in unknown destinations.[11]

In addition, millions of weapons remained in Pakistan and Afghanistan after the Soviet withdrawal.

It was difficult, if not impossible, for the United States to control how the weapons they supplied were used, and by whom. For example, in late 1989 the CIA quietly conveyed its concerns to the Indian government that that the sniper rifles it provided to the *Mujahedeen* might be diverted to Kashmiri militants and used against Indian officials. The CIA also lost control of Stinger missiles provided through this pipeline (see Chapter 6). Moreover, in the early 1990s, the pipeline allowed Pakistan to arm the Taliban with left-over AKs, contributing to the Taliban's rapid military success. In late 1994, the Taliban 'took possession of 18,000 Kalashnikovs from an arms dump in Pasha, a move which was considered pivotal to their success in eventually controlling the majority of the country'. The Taliban was also believed to have received US arms from Pakistan and Saudi Arabian sources in autumn 1996.[12]

The legacy of the massive aid program shaped events in Afghanistan and elsewhere for years afterwards. For example, many of the twelve training camps set up by Osama bin Laden in the 1990s were remnants of CIA centres established during the war in Afghanistan to train the *Mujahedeen* in the use of various weapons, guerrilla warfare, and urban sabotage. The British and American governments believe bin Laden built at least twelve training camps along the border with Pakistan, which taught weapons use and terrorist tactics. US officials estimate that, from 1996, between fifteen and twenty thousand people, from fifty countries, passed through these camps. L'Houssaine Kherchtou, who testified at the trial of four of the men thought to be responsible for the 1998 bombings of the US embassies in Tanzania and Kenya, said that in his first two months of study at the al-Farouq camp near Khost he had 'a month of training with pistols, rifles and sub-machine-guns, followed by two weeks learning about mines, explosives and grenades, then two weeks on anti-aircraft weapons'.[13]

The Cold War decision to arm the *Mujahedeen* continues to contribute to violence and conflict in the region. Arms bazaars remain in towns along the border between Pakistan and Afghanistan, where enormous quantities and varieties of weapons are readily available. The pipeline's networks and routes help the flow of both drugs and weapons – an illicit and continuing trade.[14] For these reasons, Afghanistan is a powerful reminder of the dangers associated with the uncontrolled proliferation of small arms and light weapons.

the middle east: hotbed of conflict

Small arms can affect the same region in very different ways as evidenced by the cases of Israel and Iraq. In the armed struggle between Israel and the Palestinians, small arms are misused by armed groups, terrorists and government forces. Between September 29, 2000 and February 28, 2006 (the on-going *Intifada*) more than 3400 Palestinians and nearly a thousand Israelis were killed, many by small arms. Between January 1, 2003 and October 14, 2005 alone, 155 people were killed and another 939 wounded in the Gaza Strip; thirty of those killed and 134 of the injured were children.[15]

The small arms and light weapons used by Palestinian fighters come from a variety of sources. In May 2004, the *Jerusalem Post* reported that militant groups were bringing in weapons via tunnels between Egypt and Palestine. Katyusha rockets, mortars, shoulder-mounted anti-aircraft missiles, anti-tank grenades, explosives, ammunition and rifles from Egypt, Iraq, Sudan and Libya have streamed through these tunnels, built to evade the Israeli Navy, which has become more effective at intercepting seaborne smugglers. Other reports note that most of the three thousand Kalashnikovs in a Hamas shipment – giving the group a total of ten thousand weapons – were possibly intended for use by thousands of new recruits. An Israeli officer claimed that terrorist groups are also emptying Sinai arms dumps in Gaza.[16]

Regardless of their origin, the number of weapons in Gaza, where armed gangs and militant groups freely operate, is destabilizing the region. Cross-border violence, deadly terrorist attacks, fear, insecurity and lawlessness is widespread. Officials on both sides are looking for solutions to the widespread misuse of small arms. For example, in September 2005, the Palestinian authorities implemented a ban on public displays of weapons, in an effort to create an environment of law and order.[17]

Human rights advocates have also documented the irresponsible use of small arms by Israeli government forces:

> Israeli security forces, often relying on small arms, have resorted to excessive and indiscriminate use of lethal force, such as when they have fired on rock-throwing demonstrators, employed deadly force against Palestinian civilians to enforce curfews or returned fire indiscriminately in response to Palestinian fire. In addition, Israeli soldiers have recklessly exposed civilians to danger by coercing them, sometimes at gunpoint, to perform life-endangering acts that assisted Israeli military operations.[18]

In short, the continued proliferation of weapons in Palestine and Israel allows violence to continue and is an obstacle to a peaceful solution to the conflict.

The proliferation and misuse of small arms have also had profound effects on conflict resolution, reconstruction and stability in Iraq. In the months before the 2003 war, the number of small arms in Iraq increased as people acquired guns and ammunition in preparation for the anticipated chaos. When the Baathist regime collapsed, troops were ill-prepared to secure the country's numerous weapons stockpiles. Fleeing Iraqi soldiers often abandoned the armories they were guarding (although some took their weapons home for self-protection). Some Iraqis stole unsecured weapons for protection against escalating violence and others were stolen by criminals. The increased availability of guns is reflected in their cost before and after the conflict. Before the Coalition invasion, an AK cost between $200 and $300 and a handgun cost $600. During the initial invasion, in March 2003, prices fell by fifty per cent. Although the sale of guns has been banned in Iraq since the toppling of Saddam Hussein, weapons are readily available and black market sales have increased, most noticeably before the 2005 elections.[19]

The easy availability and frequent misuse of weapons has fueled violence, insecurity and fear in Iraq. Tens of thousands of Iraqis have been killed or injured, countless others terrorized and coalition and Iraqi soldiers carry out their missions at great risk of death or injury. In the first eight months of 2004 alone, there were three thousand gun-related deaths in Baghdad. Between May 2003 (the declared end of major operations) and February 2006, an average of two American soldiers died every day in Iraq, and thousands more have been injured, many from attacks using small arms and light weapons. Patrols are threatened and vehicles and buildings damaged by small arms, which, together with improvised explosive devices (IED), are the favored tools of Iraqi insurgents, terrorists and criminals. An estimated ninety per cent of the 24,000 new Iraqi businesses lie idle because they are unable to secure a workforce and supplies to get started. Small business owners have complained that the lack of security and unreliable electricity, among other factors, have made it difficult to conduct business at all.[20]

At first, the proliferation of small arms was not a high priority of the US military, which was preoccupied with finding evidence of weapons of mass destruction and myriad other post-conflict tasks. However, by June 2003, US forces recognized the acute danger posed by the loose weapons and began to establish collection programs. A US policy allowed Iraqi citizens to keep one gun of up to 7.62 mm – which could therefore include Kalashnikov assault rifles – in their homes for protection (carrying weapons outside of one's home required special permission), but required them to surrender all other weapons. This policy resulted in many weapons remaining in circulation. Failure to comply was punishable by a $1000 fine or a year in prison. The initial results fell far short of hopes of promoting a 'safe and secure environment'; twelve days into the program, only approximately 650 weapons had been handed over.[21] The large number of weapons remaining in circulation continue to fuel violence and instability.

In September 2003, US General John Abizaid estimated that it would take five years to destroy the ordnance that US forces had then recovered. However, in the following six months, US troops discovered another eight thousand arms caches, and were discovering more every week, making Abizaid's five year estimate seem like an understatement. Compounding the problem is the steady stream of weapons entering Iraq across its insecure borders with Syria and Iran.[22]

By May 2004, an estimated 600,000–700,000 tons of weapons were still either in circulation or held in insecure stockpiles. That month, the United States again tried to sop up some of the weapons with an eight-day gun buy-back program, offering amnesty and cash payments for weapons. An AK-47 was valued at $125. Approximately $350,000 was paid out each day for a variety of small arms and light weapons, including surface to air missiles, rifles and ammunition. Iraqis were again not required to turn in all their weapons and some exploited the program by buying weapons on the black market and selling them to the US military for a profit. Others turned in old weapons and used the cash to purchase newer models on the black market. While the buy-back was seen by some officials and Iraqis as a symbolic achievement, it did little to reduce the actual number of small arms in Iraq, or to improve security on a large scale. As of November 2004, US forces had destroyed 240,000 tons of munitions and secured an additional 160,000 tons. Despite this progress, as much as 250,000 tons of weaponry remains unaccounted for.[23]

The violence in Iraq is a complex problem but there is little doubt that peace will be elusive as long as the proliferation and misuse of small arms continues. The conflict will continue to rage until multiple strategies are pursued, including gaining control over the immense quantities of weapons within the country and ensuring that they are used exclusively for lawful purposes.

africa: continent of sorrow

Across Africa, weapons are recycled from country to country, devastating one community after another. Sometimes these weapons move with the fighters and sometimes they are bought by black marketeers and sold to the highest bidder. Nowhere are the effects of recycled weapons more apparent than in war-ravaged western Africa. The actions of Charles Taylor, in particular, have been extremely detrimental to the peoples of western African countries, where thousands have been killed in two decades of fighting.

Taylor began his public career as head of the Liberian General Services Agency, the agency in charge of Liberia's budget. In 1983, President Samuel Doe charged him with embezzlement and he fled to the United States, where he was held in a Massachusetts prison under a Liberian extradition order. Taylor managed to escape and returned to Africa in 1989. From Côte d'Ivoire, he launched an armed rebellion against Doe's regime, which culminated in a civil war that lasted nearly a decade, claiming more than 250,000 lives and ruining countless more.[24]

In 1991, while waging civil war in Liberia, Charles Taylor established an informal alliance with Foday Sankoh, leader of the Revolutionary United Front (RUF) guerrillas of Sierra Leone. Taylor supplied RUF fighters with weapons, in exchange for diamonds from rebel-controlled mines. The Liberian civil war ended in a peace treaty in 1995, and in 1997 Taylor was elected President. Taylor used his position to spread instability across western Africa. He armed two Ivorian rebel groups – the Popular Movement for the Ivorian Great West and the Movement for Justice and Peace – using them to destabilize the Ivorian government, install a ruler more amenable to his interests and defeat the Guinean-supported militia, Liberians United for Reconciliation and Democracy.[25]

Taylor used the lucrative Liberian timber industry (alleged to be little more than a front for illegal arms trading and diamond smuggling), to fund both RUF guerrillas in Sierra Leone and his own forces. Arms brokers from as far away as China organized shipments, which arrived through Liberian ports controlled by the Oriental Timber Company and Maryland Wood Processing Industries, both of which were controlled by Taylor and protected by government-backed militias. The brokers arranged arms purchases, mostly Chinese-made AK series rifles, which traveled from eastern Europe via Libya, Nigeria and France. Between June and August 2002, the Yugoslavian government alone sent more than two hundred tons of small arms (mostly rifles and missile launchers) and ammunition to Liberia.[26]

In 1999, Taylor's activities came under the scrutiny of the United Nations after he was accused of smuggling arms and diamonds in violation of UN sanctions first established in 1992. The UN imposed further sanctions in 2001, and in June 2003, Taylor was indicted by a UN-backed war crimes court in Sierra Leone on seventeen counts of war crimes and crimes against humanity, including unlawful killings, sexual violence, forced conscription of child soldiers, forced labor and attacks on UN peacekeeping personnel. In March 2006, the charges were consolidated into eleven counts. He avoided arrest and fled to asylum in Nigeria in August 2003.[27] In March 2006, Taylor attempted to flee Nigeria, but was caught and extradited to Liberia, where he was arrested and sent to Sierra Leone to stand trial at the UN war crimes tribunal. As this book was in its final stages, in April 2006, the tribunal was considering moving Taylor's trial to the International Criminal Court in The Hague, for fear that his presence in Sierra Leone could be destabilizing.

The protracted conflicts in Liberia and Sierra Leone have ravaged the populations of these countries. People have been terrorized by gun-wielding rebels and subjected to systematic human rights abuses. Nearly half the population of Liberia and a quarter of Sierra Leone's have fled from their homes. The infrastructures of both countries have been obliterated and their populations face widespread unemployment and illiteracy.[28]

Unfortunately, western Africa is not the only area to have suffered from small arms proliferation and misuse on the continent. The 1994 genocide in Rwanda is but one example of the devastation that plagues the Great Lakes region. While most of the 800,000 Rwandans killed in the 100 days of the genocide were slaughtered with machetes and other bladed weapons, the murderers were assisted by AK-47 wielding soldiers and supporters, who blocked escape routes and threatened observers. The Kalashnikovs wielded by the genocidaires were supplied by a variety of countries, including France, Egypt, South Africa, Russia and Romania and other former Warsaw Pact countries.[29] Rwanda has begun to recover, but many perpetrators of the genocide continue to fight in the conflicts in Burundi and the Democratic Republic of the Congo.

tools of terror

Photos and video clips of terrorists often show them carrying and using guns such as the AK-47. Indeed, of the roughly 175 terrorist incidents identified in the 2003 US State Department's Patterns of Global Terrorism report, approximately half were perpetrated with small arms and light weapons.[30] But why are these weapons so attractive to terrorists? Because they are deadly, accurate, portable, easily hidden and readily available.

Even the least sophisticated, small-scale, terrorist incidents exploit the advantages of small arms. As Terry Gander has put it:

> In terror situations, the use of firearms can be every bit as effective as a bomb. The mere sight of a determined guerrilla appearing armed in a crowded environment is enough to cause all manner of panic and dismay in any crowd. If the weapon involved is something as menacing in appearance as an assault rifle or sub-machine-gun, the effect of its appearance alone can be every bit as extreme as the weapon firing; even the sight of a pistol can have a numbing effect on group behaviour ...'[31]

In 2002 alone, the world witnessed two high-profile terrorist incidents involving small arms and light weapons. In October, the Moscow Palace of Culture Theatre was occupied by fifty Chechen militants wielding guns, including Kalashnikovs, and explosives. They held some 750 hostages in a three-day siege. The militants were led by Movsar Barayev, a twenty-four year old leader of the Islamic Battalions. They identified themselves as members of the 29th Division of the Chechen Army. A month later and a continent away, two SA-7 *Grail* shoulder-fired surface-to-air missiles were fired at an Arkia (Israel) Airlines Boeing 757 as it took off from Mombasa airport in Kenya. The failed attack was believed to be the work of al Qaeda-linked terrorists. The widespread availability and ease of use of small arms and light weapons allows even unorganized perpetrators to engage in terrorism. In September 2005, a father and son hijacked a plane in Colombia using two grenades that they had managed to smuggle past airport security. Neither father nor son was associated with an armed group – they were protesting against the government's refusal to compensate the father for an injury sustained when he was mistakenly shot during a 1991 police drug raid.[32]

Terrorists obtain weapons from the same sources and routes as other illegal purchasers – including the black market, theft and craft production. In Bangladesh, for example, government-identified terrorists were discovered to be trafficking craft-produced weapons bought on the black market. Terrorists are also able to acquire weapons by utilizing existing legal channels and exploiting loopholes in national arms laws and export regulations. A manual, *How I can train myself for jihad*, discovered at an Islamic terrorist organization training centre in Kabul, highlights the easy availability of guns in the United States and calls on members of al Qaeda living in the United States to obtain weapons, preferably the AK-47 or its variants, from gun shows and gun shops. A 2003 Congressional Research Service report found that 'foreign terrorists could exploit and appear to have exploited in limited cases, the general availability of firearms in the United States to carry out terrorist attacks in the United States or abroad [and acquired these weapons] through either legal or illegal channels'.[33]

A 2001 report by the Brady Centre to Prevent Gun Violence found further evidence that terrorists can buy assault rifles and high-capacity ammunition magazines easily, that gun kits are purchased via mail order, that corrupt gun dealers provide weapons to would-be terrorists and that gun shows are sources of illegal weapons purchases. The report highlighted several attempts by individuals to ship US weapons to foreign terrorists. For example, Ali Boumelhem was convicted on weapons related and conspiracy charges, for purchasing weapons at gun shows in Michigan in order to send them to the terrorist group *Hezbollah*. The absence of federal or state laws requiring private sellers to conduct background checks on buyers allowed this convicted felon to buy weapons. In another harrowing case, a member of the Irish Republican Army, Conor Claxton, was sentenced to five years in jail in September 2000 for shipping guns to Northern Ireland. Claxton worked with a legal gun dealer, Edward Bluestein, to purchase weapons without filing the required paperwork. In exchange, Bluestein received an extra $50 per gun. Only after the British authorities intercepted the packages and traced the guns back to Bluestein was the smuggling ring uncovered.[34]

Small arms proliferation also supports terrorism indirectly. The proliferation and misuse of weapons puts peacekeepers in danger, reduces business opportunities, impedes the operations of humanitarian and relief organizations and hampers sustainable development. The resulting insecurity, economic stagnation and deprivation breeds alienation and frustration in distressed people, which terrorists and criminals exploit to recruit new members and perpetuate cultures of violence.

killing peace

Clearly, the proliferation and misuse of small arms devastates countries at war, but these weapons also harm countries at peace, taking tens of thousands of lives and draining community resources. In fact, the death rate from gun-related suicides and murders is higher in some 'peaceful' countries than in those at war. An Inter-American Development Bank estimate put the direct and indirect costs of gun violence in Latin America at between $140 and $170 billion a year during the 1990s. In Brazil, the cost of gun violence is approximately ten per cent of the annual gross domestic product and in Colombia, it is closer to twenty-five per cent.[35]

There are an estimated 17.5 million guns in Brazil; ninety per cent are believed to be in civilian hands and fifty per cent are held illegally. Approximately 160,000 illegal weapons are available in Rio de Janeiro alone. More people have been killed by guns in Brazil during the last ten years than in any other country, including countries at war. In 2004, more than 36,000 people were shot to death – one death every fifteen minutes – according to government statistics. Well-armed gangs, mostly using handguns, have terrorized Rio de Janeiro, particularly the poorest areas – the *favelas*. While the police have stepped up weapons seizures and interdiction efforts, gun violence remains high and the gun culture is becoming more pervasive. The average age of gang leaders is falling as more and more youths are turning to the gun for power and protection. Guns are the major cause of death for Brazilian males aged between fifteen and twenty-four and kill more people than motor vehicle injuries. In a referendum in October 2005, Brazilians voted on a proposal to criminalize civilian possession of guns and ammunition.[36] Although the referendum failed (sixty-four to thirty-six percent), nonetheless, nearly thirty-six million people voted for a ban. The vote was the first of its kind and may serve as a model for other countries plagued by high rates of gun violence.

The United States has an estimated 230–280 million guns – almost one per person. Since 1970, over one million people – more than 30,000 people annually – have died from gunshot wounds. These weapons have also exacted a high economic toll on US society. Studies in the 1990s estimated the costs of medical care for firearm-related disability, injury and death as being between $100 million and $155 million a year, with a cost of approximately $17,000 for each injury, up to eighty per cent of which was paid for by US taxpayers. However, the cost of gun violence extends beyond medical care. As a doctor told the United Nations in 2001, the impact of gun violence 'extends to police services, lost productivity, rehabilitation, psychological support for victims and their families and children growing up without parents'.[37]

stemming the flow of small arms

We sell weapons not for offensive but for defense purposes and this is done in strict compliance with international standards and regulations.

Mikhail Kalashnikov[1]

Unlike other weapons, no international control system governs small arms – and no single treaty would be able to address the myriad problems of their proliferation and misuse. What is needed is a multi-layered approach that curtails the flow of guns to conflict zones and criminals in peaceful nations, while taking into account the legitimate needs of states, law-abiding civilian firearms ownership and other appropriate uses. Policies and programs should encourage continued focus on small arms issues, prevent illegal transfers and halt the actions of abusive users. The United Nations will assuredly be an important forum for these efforts but local community structures, national governments and regional organizations will also play an important role.

This chapter describes national, regional and international strategies for controlling small arms, addresses some of the obstacles and challenges to their implementation, and provides insights on the future of control efforts.

beginning a movement

During the Cold War, nuclear, biological and chemical weapons dominated international policy agendas and arms control efforts. Until the early 1990s, if countries were interested in the control of conventional weapons, it was predominantly heavy weapons that received attention. For example, the UN Register of Conventional Arms – a voluntary mechanism for sharing information on imports, exports and procurement of some weapon systems – and the Wassenaar Arrangement, the goal of which is to promote greater responsibility in conventional arms and dual use exports, both focus primarily on heavy conventional weapons. Small arms were often left out of these efforts.

The awarding of the 1997 Nobel Peace Prize to the *International Campaign to Ban Landmines* gave impetus to more co-ordinated action on small arms control, although non-governmental organizations (NGOs) and the United Nations had already been working on this issue. NGOs saw the United Nations as one of the key forums for co-ordinated international action on gun violence and small arms control. In 1995, Secretary-General, Boutros Boutros Ghali, published his *Supplement to an agenda for peace* which identified small arms as an issue of interest for the UN. In the section on arms control and disarmament, he defined the concept of micro-disarmament as 'practical disarmament in the context of the conflicts the United Nations is actually dealing with and of the weapons, most of them light weapons, that are actually killing people in the hundreds of thousands'. He went on to observe that the 'contemporary significance of micro-disarmament is demonstrated by the enormous proliferation of automatic assault weapons, anti-personnel mines and the like'.[2] In a few short sentences Boutros Ghali identified small arms pro-liferation as a serious security threat and spurred the international community into action.

Soon after the *Supplement*'s publication, the United Nations began work in earnest. In 1996, a UN Panel of Governmental Experts began discussions that culminated in a plan for future UN work on small arms. In their 1999 report to the General Assembly, the Panel proposed that the UN should host a conference on small arms. The UN Group of Governmental Experts, comprised of officials from twenty-three countries, did the groundwork which, together with other initiatives, culminated in the 2001 UN *Conference on the illicit trade of small arms and light weapons in all its aspects.* The Conference resulted in a Programme of Action (PoA) to encourage the pursuit of strategies to reduce the proliferation and misuse of small arms and light weapons at the national, regional and international levels. The strategies are divided into ten pillars:

- national points of contact (individuals within government) and national co-ordination agencies (groups may include civil society as well as government departments);
- legislation, regulation and administrative procedures;
- criminalization regimes;
- stockpile management and security;
- weapons collection and disposal;
- export, import and transfer controls and regulations;
- brokering;
- marking, tracing and record-keeping;
- disarmament, demobilization and reintegration of ex-combatants; and
- assistance and international co-operation in tackling different aspects and consequences of the illicit small arms and light weapons trade in all its aspects.[3]

Meetings were held in 2003 and 2005 to assess progress made in implementing the PoA, and a review conference took place in June–July 2006 that intended to examine progress on implementation and revisit the PoA to determine what future action, if any, the United Nations should take. However, the conference failed to reach any agreement whatsoever.

While the PoA is a step forward, it has several limitations. PoA items are voluntary – states are not legally bound to comply with them, there are no enforcement mechanisms and the mandate to cover the 'illicit trade in all its aspects' is ambiguous. As a result, implementation efforts vary widely. Some measures have been broadly implemented while compliance with others remains limited to countries with sophisticated export control systems. Some countries lack even basic export control systems and do not have the capacity to develop the requisite legislation, regulations and enforcement mechanisms to implement the recommendations. Even the simplest obligations are often implemented at a glacial pace. For example, in 2003, only 111 states had designated national points of contact on PoA implementation (which amounts to naming a point person within the government). Two years later, that number had increased to 143, but still fell short of universal implementation. Likewise, in 2003 thirty-seven states had designated national co-ordination agencies, which increased only to seventy-nine by 2005.[4]

States have also moved slowly to develop policies for controlling small arms exports. In 2003, 105 states had some kind of legislation or procedure but by 2005, only two more countries had been added to this list. Further, of these 107 states, only thirty-seven have legislation requiring an assessment of the risk of diversion of exports, only fifty-six require use of authenticated end-user certificates, and only twenty-five have legislation requiring them to notify the original exporting state when retransferring previously imported arms.[5] These statistics are not encouraging.

Beyond the PoA, the United Nations has addressed various aspects of small arms proliferation in some thirty Security Council and General Assembly resolutions. For more than a decade, these resolutions have influenced control efforts both within and outside the UN and are a barometer of its influence. Nearly all the resolutions encourage regional initiatives and the inclusion of civil society in developing programs and policies. They also urge donor states to support efforts in other countries and encourage continued attention from the UN. The Secretary-General has produced regular reports and the Security Council has imposed arms embargoes on those countries involved in significant armed conflicts and human rights abuses.

regional small arms and light weapons initiatives

States can more easily reach consensus in smaller groups and when dealing with issues that affect their particular region. As a result, regional organizations have been able to develop meaningful and sometimes quite far-reaching small arms policies. While regional agreements and initiatives may only affect a particular region, they can serve as models and test cases for future international small arms efforts.

In November 1997, the Organization of American States (OAS) adopted the *Inter-American Convention against the Illicit Manufacturing of and Trafficking in Firearms, Ammunition, Explosives and other Related Materials* (CIFTA). The convention calls on member states to establish strong export controls, mark small arms at the time of manufacture and when transferred, and co-operate on small arms trafficking investigations. The convention has been ratified by most, but not all, OAS member states. Hold-outs include Canada, the United States, the Dominican Republic, Haiti and Jamaica. Some diplomats believe that the United States' vast economic and diplomatic influence makes US ratification particularly important and that without it, the treaty will eventually be 'sapped of its credibility'. However, even with universal ratification, the convention would not be a panacea, as the problems that contribute to small arms proliferation are too numerous and diverse for a single solution. To have a comprehensive and lasting effect, implementation of the OAS Firearms Convention must be pursued together with other initiatives.[6]

Two African small arms control initiatives are legally binding and go further than current international efforts. The first is the *Nairobi Protocol*, which seeks to reduce gun trafficking and violence in east Africa. The protocol requires its members[a] to ensure their national laws cover various aspects of small arms control,

[a] Nairobi Protocol members are: Burundi, Democratic Republic of Congo, Djibouti, Ethiopia, Eritrea, Kenya, Rwanda, Seychelles, Sudan, Tanzania and Uganda.

including their manufacture, marking, identification, registration, possession, brokering, import, export, transit, transport and transfer; a ban on civilian ownership of automatic and semi-automatic rifles; and the regulation of security companies. The member states are also required to maintain inventories of state-owned small arms, so they may be effectively traced, and develop disposal or destruction regulations and practices for surplus and confiscated weapons. In September 2005, the member states agreed to set up a legislative drafting team to help states in the development and harmonization of national regulations.[7]

The second African initiative is the *Southern African Development Community Protocol on Firearms, Ammunition and Related Materials*, which is designed to enhance national controls on arms trafficking and possession. The protocol came into force on November 8, 2004, and regional standards on marking were developed in July 2004. The Protocol countries[b] are at different stages of developing national institutions to co-ordinate implementation and constructing national action plans.

States have taken other collective steps towards strengthening export controls. For example, a UK initiative on export controls emerged from a conference held in London in January 2003. Representatives from forty-nine countries and delegates from international, regional and non-governmental organizations focused on ways to strengthen the PoA, establish national guidelines (especially in states that had few or weak regulations) and build a consensus on arms exports and brokering activities. These instruments and institutions are important tools in the ever-growing policy toolbox for small arms control.

national practices

National arms control policies vary enormously. Some nations have extensive laws regulating the export, internal circulation, and

[b] SADC Protocol members are: Angola, Botswana, Democratic Republic of Congo, Lesotho, Malawi, Mauritius, Mozambique, Namibia, Seychelles, South Africa, Swaziland, Tanzania, Zambia and Zimbabwe.

possession of guns, while others have virtually none. Even though one of the goals of the UN PoA was to encourage countries to review and ultimately strengthen policies and regulations for control, many national laws remain weak.

The United States is often hailed as having impressive and comprehensive export controls. American law requires, among other provisions, licenses for most arms exports, oversight of the transfer of arms, the prohibition of the transfer of weapons without state permission and regulations on decommissioning and disposal.[c] The United States has two monitoring programs to ensure that weapons are received by the intended user and that they are used in compliance with US law. US brokering laws are particularly strong and, unlike in most countries, apply to American citizens no matter where they do business. The State Department's Small Arms and Light Weapons destruction program also helps other countries destroy surplus or obsolete weapons and improve security over those that remain.

Canadian laws and regulations[d] criminalize the illicit manufacture, trade and possession of small arms, including the violation of UN arms embargoes. Although it has no explicit brokering legislation, the activities of brokers are indirectly regulated by other laws. Canada is a leader in the UN small arms process and is a major donor to multilateral and bilateral control initiatives. Among other efforts, it has served as lead government in the NATO *Partnership for Peace* project in Albania and contributed to NATO's *South East Europe Initiative*. Canada is also one of the forces behind the human security approach, which focuses on the people affected by weapons, not just the weapons themselves.[8]

Although many other countries have strong small arms laws, major gaps in national policies remain. As mentioned earlier, only thirty-seven countries assess the risk of diversion before authorizing

[c] Relevant US laws and regulations include the Arms Export Control Act, the Foreign Assistance Act of 1961, and the International Traffic in Arms Regulations (ITAR).

[d] Relevant Canadian law is contained in the Firearms Act, the Defense Production Act, the Controlled Goods Program, and the Export and Import Permits Act, which includes the Automatic Firearms Country Control List.

exports and only fifty-six require authenticated end-user certificates.[9] End-user certificates increase transparency and accountability by helping governments to ensure their exported weapons reach the intended recipients. Without universal adoption of these safeguards, guns will continue to flow into the hands of criminals.

non-governmental organizations

Since the early 1990s, universities, think tanks and other organizations have taken an increasing interest in gun violence and the arms trade. As weapons proliferated, so did the articles, analyses and policy suggestions on how to curtail the burgeoning threat. Today, NGOs carry out significant research into the effects and uses of small arms, develop solutions and monitor government policies and practice.

Like their government counterparts, NGOs operate at the international, national and local levels. The *International Action Network on Small Arms* was launched to co-ordinate action and facilitate the exchange of information. One of the most active NGOs at the national level is *Viva Rio* in Rio de Janeiro, which has worked with Brazilian government officials to improve national laws and regulations, and to collect and destroy surplus and illicit small arms. In June 2001, 100,000 guns were publicly destroyed in one of several simultaneous events held on the first annual international gun destruction day. In July 2002, another ten thousand guns were destroyed and in 2003, a further five thousand. These efforts raised awareness of the widespread proliferation of firearms and put pressure on the Brazilian Congress to implement strong gun control legislation. The *National Voluntary Firearms Handover* campaign in 2004 recovered nearly 250,000 weapons in six months, three times its target. In response, the President of Brazil extended the program for six months, with a new target of 400,000 guns, which was also met.[10] The culmination of Vivo Rio's campaign was the October 2005 national referendum on a proposed law to prohibit commerce in small arms and ammunition. While the measure failed, the NGO campaign to support it raised awareness and served as an example for other NGOs around the world.

Awareness-raising is one of the most important activities in which NGOs regularly engage. For example, after the 2001 UN Conference, the *Philippines Action Network on Small Arms* ran a public education and awareness campaign in three districts particularly hard-hit by armed violence and crime. Films, photos and other educational materials demonstrating the human cost of arms abuse in the Philippines helped communities deal with the effects.[11]

NGOs also contribute substantially to the development of regional small arms agreements. For years, the Economic Community of West African States[e] (ECOWAS) has discussed making its moratorium on small arms permanent and legally binding. Rather than waiting for states to take action, the West Africa Action Network on Small Arms (WAANSA), with the support of Oxfam, developed its own version of a legally-binding treaty. In March 2005, a coalition of West African civil society groups and representatives of the ECOWAS countries' National Commissions on small arms adopted a *Draft Convention on Small Arms and Light Weapons.* Using the original 1998 ECOWAS moratorium as its foundation, the convention improves upon the original moratorium by addressing the local manufacture of small arms and highlighting the ways in which small arms affect women and men differently and on the local manufacture of small arms.[12] On October 5, 2005, WAANSA presented the Draft Convention to the ECOWAS Secretariat. The Secretariat approved the Convention at a summit meeting on June 14, 2006.

Even though governments and NGOs work together successfully on small arms issues, the partnership is often fraught with tension. For many states, civil society input into security matters is novel and problematic. NGOs are often forced to push

---

[e] ECOWAS member states are: Benin, Burkina Faso, Cape Verde, Côte d'Ivoire, the Gambia, Ghana, Guinea, Guinea-Bissau, Liberia, Mali, Mauritania, Niger, Nigeria, Senegal, Sierra Leo.

governments to adopt lower standards than they advocate, simply to see progress made. In the meantime, NGOs advocate specific steps for states to undertake, including:

- legally binding international treaties on arms brokering;
- marking and tracing and arms export criteria;
- development of transparency mechanisms for small arms exports and imports;
- expansion of assistance programs to states seeking more effective implementation;
- enforcement of arms export laws, regulations and procedures, including providing increased law enforcement and export control training.

Among several other countries, the United States, Russia and China have opposed these proposals, for various reasons. They fear such initiatives will encroach on their sovereignty, infringe on current national practices and limit their future freedom of action. Beyond prerogatives for state practice, some governments argue that it is their responsibility to develop and implement policy, not the international community's or civil society's. Despite government opposition, NGOs remain undeterred and continue to press their positions in national, regional and international forums.

obstacles to action

The United Nations has become a key venue for advancing multi-lateral controls on small arms proliferation and misuse.[13] However, the sometimes slow and unimaginative nature of the UN process can hinder action. Many government representatives come from a nuclear arms control background and are accustomed to focusing on the control of supply to prevent proliferation. This perspective colors the views of these diplomats, who rarely consider the many other different strategies for stemming weapons proliferation. Moreover, the UN's consensus-based decision making method can result in a 'lowest common denom-inator' outcome as, to reach an agreement, states must acquiesce to those unwilling to adopt the highest standards.

The approach to the problem also hinders action. Governments often pursue small arms control efforts that address either legal or illegal transfers but not both. The United States, for example, has consistently objected to international restrictions on civil ownership, the legal trade and manufacture of weapons and the sale of weapons to organizations other than governments. These objections are both politically and economically motivated. In general, many arms-producing states view arms sales as an important source of revenue and a valuable foreign policy tool for influencing a recipient state's policies or actions. Therefore, governments often shy away from initiatives that might circumscribe the legal transfer of weapons. However, legal arms sales are a major source (through diversion or theft) for black market weapons and therefore must be considered when devising strategies for reducing illicit arms transfers.

Many small arms control initiatives have been left off the policy agenda, either because the plate is seen as too full or the initiative as too controversial. One of the most contentious issues is the supply of weapons to non-state actors (insurgents, terrorists or other armed groups). Many governments, particularly those that face armed opposition to their rule, are keen to ensure that only states can receive weapons. However, the United States and other countries consistently object to proposals for a complete ban on transfers to non-state actors for two main reasons: they are often leery of externally imposed constraints on their foreign policy and they occasionally arm guerrilla forces to advance key foreign policy objectives. American resistance to such bans has increased since the terrorist attacks of September 11, 2001. Immediately after the attacks, Secretary of State Colin Powell stated that the United States would provide arms to groups such as the Afghan Northern Alliance and Iraqi opposition groups. This policy ensured that a total ban on arming non-state actors would not reach consensus in the near future, even though the United States has demanded the end of transfers of MANPADS and nuclear material to non-state actors, and has pushed through agreements that include support for such targeted bans at the UN and in other international fora.

Although the United Nations has been instrumental in establishing a global small arms framework, local, national, regional and other global organizations may eventually replace it as the focal point of small arms action. However, programs at these levels will require significant changes in national policies. To be effective, countries will have to share more law enforcement and intelligence and rigorously pursue collaborative financial, logistical and technical programs.

next steps

Three proposed treaties would, if adopted and widely implemented, move the world a step closer toward universal controls of small arms and light weapons. These treaties address the marking and tracing of weapons, arms brokering and export controls.

marking and tracing

Weapons flow quickly from one country to another and it is often difficult to ascertain where they originated, which countries they traveled through and where they end up. One way to increase transparency and accountability of weapons transfers is to mark weapons when they are produced, exported and imported. When the origin and transfer routes of weapons can be identified, it becomes easier to work out how and when they got into the hands of unintended users and identify those responsible for supplying and diverting the weapons.

The marking of small arms is, to some extent, covered at the international level in the UN Firearms Protocol, but there is no single system for marking or tracing small arms and light weapons. The PoA called for a feasibility study on the development of international standards and for the unique, appropriate and reliable marking of all small arms at their production. In June 2005, after a series of meetings on marking and tracing, governments agreed to a political, non-binding document that seeks to establish minimum standards for marking and an international mechanism for tracing weapons in order to increase international co-operation. The agreement has been criticized, both by NGOs and states, for being weaker than other legally-binding national and regional standards and for missing key elements, such as standardized markings and the marking of ammunition. Some NGOs, led by the *Groupe de Recherche et d'Information sur la Paix et la Sécurité*, have developed a *Draft Convention on Marking, Registration and Tracing* that addresses some of these concerns.

brokering

Brokering – the private dealing in weapons – is an under-regulated area of the small arms trade. Despite the need for strict regulations on brokering, without which weapons can be illicitly transferred with impunity, only around forty countries have adopted legislation on brokering.[14] NGOs and other advocates of brokering controls are attempting to address this problem through regional agreements and implementation of the PoA.

Regional organizations are co-ordinating standards on brokering. The Southern African Development Community agreed to regulate brokering within its territories as part of its Firearms Protocol in August 2001. On November 15, 2001, the European Parliament passed a resolution calling for an international treaty on arms brokering (as well as an international treaty on the transfer of arms) and agreed to appoint a group of states to facilitate the treaty process. In June 2002, the EU countries adopted a common position, requiring the development of controls on arms brokers and the establishment of penalties for violations. In 2003, Wassenaar Arrangement and member states of the Organization for Security and Co-operation in Europe developed guidelines and best practices on arms brokering. That same year, the Organization of American States developed Model Regulations for the Control of Brokers of Firearms, Their Parts and Components and Ammunition, which provide guidelines for developing national legislation and suggest mechanisms for establishing criteria for brokering.

The PoA calls for the exploration of a possible system for developing stricter controls on brokering. However, the brokering process has been slow, to the frustration of many governments and NGOs. It was agreed – contentiously – that a UN Group of Governmental Experts would begin work on the issue after the 2006 review conference but before 2007. In the meantime, states are laying the groundwork for a possible international treaty. The Dutch and Norwegian governments have been particularly active in promoting awareness of this issue. Many NGOs are also pushing for a legally binding international convention. The US NGO Fund for Peace drafted a *Model Convention on Arms Brokering*, which contains 'provisions for a registration and licensing scheme, incentives for compliance, criminal penalties for offenders and mechanisms of improved international co-operation'.[15] It also includes measures to enlist the help of the banking, insurance and manufacturing industries. Such measures could help decrease illegal arms shipments and hold dealers accountable. Standardizing regulations will prevent dealers from exploiting differences in national laws and regulations by moving their operations from country to country. Similarly, mechanisms that strengthen international co-operation on investigations and prosecutions of arms brokering will prevent dealers from acting with impunity.

eligibility criteria

Export control laws govern the transfer of arms and identify conditions that must be met for a recipient to be eligible to receive weapons. Some states' eligibility criteria prohibit arms sales to human rights abusers, undemocratic regimes or supporters of terrorism. Currently, there are no international standards for eligibility criteria, which would, among other things, reduce arms sales to problematic recipients by strengthening standards concerning acceptable end-users, decrease under-cutting (when one country agrees to make a contentious sale after others have refused) and thereby lessen human suffering caused by ill-advised small arms transfers.

NGOs have called on states to develop a convention based on their existing obligations under international law, often referred to as 'Global Principles'. To this end, they have proposed a global *Arms Trade Treaty* (ATT), which would 'prohibit arms from being exported to destinations where they are likely to be used to commit grave human rights violations', by requiring arms trade authorizations to be based on existing international human rights and humanitarian law.[16]

In October 2005, the European Union endorsed the ATT and encouraged international participation in the initiative. This raised the number of states calling for an ATT to forty-two but the prospects for the near future are bleak. The United States, Russia and China – three of the largest arms exporters in the world – have expressed skepticism and even hostility, ensuring that if the ATT is negotiated in a setting where they have a voice, it will fail. Some countries are more enthusiastic about the British *Transfer Control Initiative* (TCI), which also calls for human rights and international humanitarian law arms export criteria but is less stringent than the ATT.

Work will continue on international legal initiatives to control these aspects of the small arms trade. Meanwhile, steps can be taken to restrain the international proliferation of small arms and light weapons through the control of supply, the management of stockpiles, the prevention of misuse and the reduction of demand.[17]

controlling supply

To counter weaknesses in national, regional and international transfer controls, states work alone and with other countries in several different ways. First, national and international arms embargoes help prevent irresponsible governments and groups from obtaining weapons, by prohibiting shipments to them through legal channels. Embargoes also send a strong diplomatic message by publicly stating that the behavior of a government requires strong condemnation. Embargoes may be imposed by the United Nations, regional organizations or by individual states. Compliance with UN and regional embargoes are rarely, if ever, enforceable but national embargoes generally have both verification and enforcement mechanisms. In January 2006, there were UN arms embargoes in place against Osama bin Laden/ al-Qaeda/the Taliban, Democratic Republic of Congo, Iraq, Côte d'Ivoire, Liberia, Rwanda, Sierra Leone and Somalia. Since 1990, the United Nations has also recommended or enacted embargoes of Afghanistan, Armenia and Azerbaijan, Ethiopia and Eritrea, and Yemen, due to ongoing conflicts.[18] However, international embargoes are often ignored, poorly monitored or inadequately enforced and weapons may find their way to countries that should not receive them. This is due to corruption or inadequate oversight and accountability. Adherence to arms embargoes must be a priority, as must the meticulous investigation of suspected violations and the prosecution of transgressors.

Second, deficiencies in national control policies and practices can lead to problems internationally. For example, beginning in 2000, Slovakia was exposed as part of an international smuggling ring providing weapons to Liberia. A loophole in Slovak law made arms deals exempt from licensing requirements if the arrangement was for repair or refurbishment of weapons. As a result, two Mi-24 *Hind* helicopters were transferred from Kyrgyzstan to Slovakia for repairs and, although they were supposed to be returned to Kyrgyzstan, they were later found in Liberia.[19] States must work together to develop strict national policies and standard international practices.

Third, the lack of oversight of weapons issued to military, police or civilian owners enables small arms to enter the black market. Many governments do not undertake regular checks of military supplies and stockpiles – which contributes to undetected theft or loss – nor maintain full records of the weapons held by various groups. Legal gun owners may not report stolen or lost weapons and, in some countries, the unregulated purchase of multiple weapons may allow them to be sold illegally. Improving the oversight of weapons would help stem the illicit flow of small arms.

Fourth, inadequate monitoring of weapons often results in their theft or diversion by suspect recipients. To counter the lack of harmonized end-use procedures among governments, common international end-use certificates should be developed and systematic end-use monitoring implemented. Weapons should be checked at export, at transit points and at their destination, and exporters should verify that weapons remain with their intended recipient. Standardized and identifiable bills of lading and other required shipping documents must be developed and used. Violations of such processes should be investigated and reported. The Swedish government has been an active proponent of creating global standards on such certificates, but their call to action has largely fallen on deaf ears.

Fifth, poor national, regional and multilateral co-operation can lead to illegal arms transfers and impunity for violators, as traffickers exploit the gaps between various national systems and regulations. National security interests or a distrust of foreign counterparts are among the reasons governments do not co-operate. Even within the same country, agencies often compete for resources, credit and information and fail to share intelligence in order to protect their own interests. Governments, law enforcement agencies, border security forces and customs officials must work together to identify and eliminate trafficking routes and apprehend violators.

taking weapons out of circulation

There are a number of ways to limit the impact of the millions of weapons currently in circulation. First, destruction of surplus or obsolete weapons is crucial. When such weapons remain in a country, they can easily find their way to the black market. For example, a Ukrainian parliamentary commission estimated that when Ukraine achieved independence in 1992, its military stocks were worth $89 billion. Over the next decade, thousands of these weapons were stolen – perhaps totaling $32 billion – and re-sold abroad, including to governments and insurgent groups in many of the world's war zones.[20]

Second, government weapons stockpiles must be effectively managed and secured. The Ukraine is a good example of a country burdened by excess weapons that it cannot adequately manage. The NATO Maintenance and Supply Agency estimates that seven million small arms and light weapons and an additional two million tons of ammunition remain stored in more than eighty depots across Ukraine. These weapons are a potential proliferation threat as the storage depots were not designed to hold quantities of this magnitude.[21] Stocks of weapons are attractive sources for theft and all practical steps should be undertaken to ensure that the weapons remain under lock and key.

Third, disarmament, demobilization and reintegration (DDR) programs often help to reduce the illicit trafficking and misuse of weapons in the hands of ex-combatants and armed gangs. While there is no one-size-fits-all approach, best practices have emerged from numerous programs around the world. Successful DDR programs emphasize the voluntary, not forced, nature of the process. Money, goods, services or skills training are often offered to former combatants in exchange for weapons. Yet, in many cases the perceived value of the weapons exceeds the value of the inducements. Some former fighters see weapons as a source of power and protection and are therefore hesitant to give them up. This was the case in Sierra Leone, where former combatants surrendered to peacekeepers but refused to turn in their weapons, despite cash incentives. A resumption of hostilities was in part attributed to the failure to disarm ex-combatants, who were able to use their hidden weapons in later battles.[22] Essential to all DDR efforts is ensuring that once weapons are collected, they are destroyed or stored safely, to prevent future theft or misuse.

DDR programs can take years to show results. The first phase of DDR in Afghanistan lasted two years; by July 2005, sixty-three thousand former combatants had been disarmed, 250 units of ex-militia members were decommissioned, 53,000 ex-combatants were given reintegration packages, and some 35,000 light and medium weapons were collected at a total cost of approximately $100 million. The DDR programs were followed by the

Disbandment of Illegal Armed Groups program aimed at reintegrating the estimated 100,000 members of approximately 1,800 illegal armed groups in Afghanistan.[23] The United Nations estimates that the reintegration programs will take another year to complete.

Fourth, because small arms have a long shelf life, they can contribute to crime or violence years after they are first used. In El Salvador, for example, more people have been killed in ten years of peace than died in the previous twelve years of war. Weapons collection and buy-back programs help to reduce proliferation and misuse by taking illegal or surplus weaponry off the streets. Such programs also raise awareness about weak gun controls and build confidence in peace-building processes in areas where insecurity is rampant. Coupled with destruction demonstrations, they symbolize positive political and social change. In Mali, Cambodia, Kosovo and Serbia, bonfires of burning small arms came to represent the ending of hostilities.[24]

Yet weapons collection programs are difficult to implement effectively and often fail to have a discernable impact on the quantity and availability of black market weapons. In some cases, they may even increase the numbers of weapons available, such as when individuals turn in unusable weapons and use the cash reward to buy new weapons. The programs may also spur increased black market sales, as people buy weapons on the black market and turn them in to the buy-back program for a higher price. That said, weapons collection programs can be effective non- and counter-proliferation tools under the right circumstances and with careful planning, and should be established when conditions permit.

ending misuse

Controlling supply and making sure guns do not end up in the wrong hands are important but there must be controls on use by legitimate owners as well, whether they be private individuals, police and security forces or non-state armed groups.

The licensing process, which regulates the ownership and use of guns by private individuals, should take into consideration, among other criteria, the applicant's history, behavior, mental health, age and knowledge of the laws about and the safe operation of weapons. Prosecutions for unlawful use and ownership must be vigorously pursued. National laws must be harmonized, particularly at the regional level. Law enforcement personnel must be properly trained in internationally accepted codes of conduct for firearms use and held fully accountable to citizens, parliament and the judiciary.

addressing demand

Most efforts to control small arms have, logically, focused on curbing the supply. However, another key control component is reducing demand. This is far more difficult, as states or individuals seek small arms for many different reasons, which vary from personal security and demonstrating power to acquiring territory or resources. Like any other commodity, demand also depends on preference, price and availability.

To be effective, demand reduction strategies must reflect the complexities of the violence in conflict areas and local realities in countries at peace or recovering from war. Government officials, community leaders and non-governmental organizations should be involved in their design, which may require considerable research. The involvement of civil society is crucial, as these groups often understand and are able to explain the local situation and the motivation of individuals. For example, in Papua New Guinea, NGO researchers found that the entrenched culture of violence makes motivation-based remedies to disarmament useless and have instead suggested raising the price of small arms to curb demand.[25]

Demand-reduction strategies should also be linked to other aspects of violence and arms reduction programs, such as reform of security services and medical care, should be built into existing programs and should combine punishment with incentives for giving up weapons.[26] Every situation is unique and the demand for weapons is shaped by particular political, societal and cultural circumstances. Regardless of the context, policies must focus on providing security and power by methods other than armed violence. Also, since guns are often used to obtain resources, demand-reduction strategies must provide other means of earning a livelihood. Such strategies may include institution building, enhancing economic development and social welfare and judicial reform.

man-portable air defense systems – the terrorists' delight

Its benign appearance belies its lethality. The Stinger missile has no gaping barrel, no steely blade, not a single telltale sign of its deadliness. In fact, it looks more like a high school science project than a super weapon capable of crippling superpowers and triggering genocide. It is much more impressive in action. When the firing trigger is pressed, the missile's launch motor ignites and it lurches out of its launch tube. Moments later, its flight motor roars to life and the Stinger chases after its prey at speeds of over 1500 mph. Locked onto the heat signature of the aircraft, the missile's sophisticated guidance system continuously adjusts its trajectory until it slams into its target 'with the kinetic force of a mid-sized car traveling at sixty miles per hour'.[1] Engines are obliterated, hydraulic and electrical lifelines are cut and wings are ripped to shreds.

Since their debut four decades ago, man-portable air defense systems (MANPADS) – and particularly Stinger missiles – have achieved iconic status amongst terrorists and insurgents. Afghan warlords refused to part with them despite black market prices that far exceeded any conceivable military value, and Colombian guerrillas reportedly offered a million dollars for a single system – enough money to cover the annual wages of thirteen hundred of their members. In recent years, this fascination has gone mainstream, particularly in the United States. US politicians – the unfailing barometers of their society's fears and obsessions – have called for the installation of electronic counter-measures on civilian aircraft, a multi-billion dollar solution to a threat that has killed fewer Americans than have been killed by zoo elephants.[2]

The next four chapters tell the story of these remarkable weapons – from their initial production in the 1960s to the current, unprecedented international campaign to rein in their proliferation. It is a harrowing tale of superpower proxy wars and trans-national super-criminals that illustrates the international community's immense capacity for both effective action and bureaucratic short-sightedness. It is also an excellent case study for illustrating the themes and concepts identified in the introduction, and applied to the AK-47 in Section One.

MANPADS have much in common with the AK-47 and other small arms. They are potent weapons and, in the hands of criminals and insurgents, an urgent security threat. They are relatively easy to use and extremely effective, transforming soldiers or insurgents from hapless victims of enemy airpower to airplane hunter-killers. In the hands of a terrorist, the same missiles are capable of crippling a $200 million commercial airliner (and with it the commercial airline industry) or bringing down a presidential plane and decapitating a government. MANPADS are also difficult to control and widely proliferated: at least twenty countries have produced them and they are in the arsenals of dozens more. They are durable, easy to smuggle and financially accessible to most serious terrorist organizations.

Yet MANPADS differ from firearms in several important ways. The estimated 100,000 missile launchers worldwide[3] are a numerical rounding error in the context of the 600 million + global small arms inventory. Most are stored in secure government arms depots, which are often monitored by guards, security cameras and intruder detection devices. Not so in the case of firearms. The black market is regularly replenished with guns stolen from leaky government arsenals, police stations, gun shops and private homes. Another key difference between MANPADS and firearms is the infrastructure, technology and expertise needed to produce them. Assembling the delicate circuitry of guided missiles requires a team of specialists with access to sophisticated equipment and facilities while knock-off AK-47s are produced by local gunsmiths in one-room workshops. MANPADS also have comparatively short shelf lives, lasting only a couple of decades if stored properly and a couple of years (or less) if mishandled.[4] Many firearms last for decades, even in harsh conditions.

These differences have profound implications for policymakers. Strategies that would barely make a dent in the proliferation of firearms could, at least in theory, have a huge impact on the MANPADS threat. At first blush, victory not only seems possible but – with the combined effort of the international community – probable. But, like with most policy issues, the problem is more vexing than it first appears. Implementing even the most straightforward control strategy is daunting, as the United States discovered when it attempted to buy back the Stinger missiles it distributed to Afghan rebels. Diplomatic and political obstacles are also formidable, as is resistance from powerful but myopic government institutions. Resource constraints, the vagaries of the policy-making process and the absence of monitoring and enforcement mechanisms in multilateral MANPADS control agreements are additional, significant challenges.

Despite these obstacles, the international community has made remarkable progress in coming to grips with the MANPADS threat, much of which dates back to November 2002, when a failed missile attack on an Israeli airliner galvanized an unprecedented international response. Since then, policymakers have fast-tracked the development of anti-missile systems for commercial airliners, negotiated international agreements on MANPADS control and destroyed thousands of surplus missiles. Such initiatives help to reduce loss, theft and diversion and protect planes when other control strategies fail.

These and other subjects are explored in the next four chapters.

the advent of the man-portable air defense system

Until the 1960s, infantrymen relied primarily on the .50 caliber machine-gun for protection against low-flying aircraft – a less than perfect defense, especially against the fast, nimble jets that were coming of age in the post-World War II era. Starting in 1948, the US military launched several projects aimed at developing an infantry anti-aircraft weapon with the range, accuracy and lethality needed to effectively engage these planes. Several years passed before Convair – a division of General Dynamics Corporation – pitched its designs for an infrared-seeking, man-portable missile. The US military embraced Convair's concept and a decade of research and testing later, the *Redeye* system – named after the infra-red-seeking 'eye' in the nose of the missile – was born. The Soviets quickly caught wind of the program and, in 1960, started their own. Aided by detailed technical descriptions of the Redeye obtained by Soviet intelligence, Russian weapons designers unveiled their own system – the SA-7 *Strela* (Arrow) – in 1968.[5]

Several other nations developed their own systems a few years later and by the Redeye's tenth anniversary in 1976, eight countries were manufacturing one of three different types of MAN-PADS: infra-red seekers, command line-of-sight (CLOS) and laser beam rider systems. Infra-red seekers quickly became the most popular, and the most proliferated, of the three types. When the operator points an infra-red seeking missile at a target, the missile's seeker locks on to one of the plane's heat sources (often an engine). After the missile is launched, it races toward the aircraft, continuously adjusting its course to keep the plane in the centre of its field of view. This process continues until the missile either hits the plane or – if the missile loses its lock on the plane's heat source – glides past it. CLOS systems are radio-controlled missiles directed to the target by an operator using a joystick. The British produced the first system, the Blowpipe, in 1975. Laser beam riders, such as the Swedish RBS-70 unveiled in 1977, follow a laser beam placed on the target by the operator.

During the 1970s, dozens of countries imported MANPADS. The Soviets sent Strelas to North Vietnam, Iraq, Egypt, North Korea, Syria and Somalia, while Saudi Arabia, Greece, Israel, Germany and other western countries received American Redeyes. By the end of the decade, MANPADS were in the arsenals of over thirty countries.[6] With so many missiles in so many different hands, it was only a matter of time before some of them ended up in the wrong hands.

the terrorists' delight

In many ways, heat-seeking MANPADS are ideal weapons for terrorists and insurgents. One missile, bought for just a few thousand dollars on the black market, can inflict serious, even catastrophic, damage on a multi-million dollar plane. The costs of damaged aircraft are often dwarfed by the indirect costs, however. MANPADS-wielding insurgents can bring an otherwise effective counter-insurgency air campaign to a grinding halt. Similarly, a well-co-ordinated attack on two or more airliners could ground commercial air traffic and send the airline industry into a financial tail-spin.

Many MANPADS are also easy to acquire, smuggle and operate. The entire system is often less than two meters long and weighs less than twenty kilograms, facilitating surreptitious transport across national borders and to attack sites. A reasonably proficient operator can set up many systems in just a few minutes – an attractive feature for insurgents, who often have only a few moments to respond to an approaching government aircraft. Quick getaways are made possible by the 'fire and forget' infra-red seeker on many MANPADS, which guides the missile to its target with no help from the operator. Recognizing this deadly combination of traits, control advocates in the US Congress started referring to MANPADS as the 'terrorist's delight'.[7]

Terrorists and insurgents wasted little time in acquiring the new weapons, which was facilitated by sympathetic governments such as that of Libyan dictator Mohammar Qaddafi. The fire-brand Colonel – who came to power in a 1969 military *coup* – spent hundreds of millions of dollars training and equipping terrorists groups in the 1970s and 80s. In 1973, he conspired with the Popular Front for the Liberation of Palestine (PFLP), a transnational Marxist-Leninist terrorist group, to shoot down an Israeli airliner in Italy. According to the US State Department, Qaddafi delivered SA-7 missile systems to members of the PFLP, who set up shop in an apartment near Rome's Fiumcino airport. Israeli intelligence uncovered the plot and notified Italian authorities, who raided the apartment and arrested five conspirators. On the balcony, they found two SA-7s 'ready to shoot down an El Al plane after take off'.[8]

Three years later, Palestinian radicals again tried to shoot down an Israeli airliner, and again they were armed with SA-7 missiles. According to the *Washington Post*, the missiles were provided by Ugandan dictator Idi Amin, an active supporter of the PLO. Even among the post-colonial dictators who ravaged sub-Saharan Africa, Amin's blood lust was legendary. Enemies of his regime, real and imagined, were executed by the thousands; at least 200,000 Ugandans were killed before his regime was toppled in 1979. Amin's bizarre behavior added to the nightmarish quality of his rule. He had 'talks' with the severed heads of victims, which he stored in a freezer, and fed the bodies of others to Nile alligators.[9]

Amin's missiles were brought to the outskirts of Nairobi Airport. There, three Palestinian conspirators waited for their target – an Israeli airliner carrying over a hundred passengers. Tipped off by Israeli intelligence, Kenyan authorities reportedly knew about the attack in advance and, like in Rome, acted in time to prevent it. The Palestinians were arrested, missiles in hand, near an airport fence. It was another victory for Israeli intelligence, but a narrow one. Had the Kenyan police been delayed, or had the Palestinians done a better job of keeping their plans a secret, the passengers on the El Al flight might have been the first casualties of a MANPADS attack on a civilian airliner.[10]

early MANPADS control efforts

Ad hoc government responses to the terrorist threat from MAN-PADS began shortly after the first missiles were developed. In November 1972, US officials paid a visit to the Soviet Embassy in Washington to complain about terrorist acquisition of Russian MANPADS. The Soviets reportedly assured the Americans that their government 'ha[d] taken and continues to take every step to insure that (missiles of this type) do not fall into the hands of irresponsible persons' – a claim that was quickly contradicted by events on the ground. After the foiled MANPADS attack in Rome a year later, American officials returned to the Soviet embassy. They reiterated their 'serious concern that Soviet missiles of this type have fallen into terrorist hands' but to no avail.[11] Soviet-designed missiles continued to find their way onto the black market.

In November 1977, West Germany launched what was probably the largest counter-MANPADS effort of the decade after authorities received letters from the Red Army Faction, a German terrorist group, threatening to 'blow up Lufthansa plane[s] in flight'. German authorities altered the take-off and landing patterns of Lufthansa passenger jets, enhanced security around German airports and requested the seventy-three nations served by Lufthansa to check all approach and departure areas around airports for terrorists armed with MANPADS.[12]

The US government initiated its first systematic, inter-agency study of the terrorist threat posed by MANPADS in 1976. It was part of a broader look at the threat of 'intermediate terrorism' (terrorism that is less destructive than nuclear or biological attacks but more destructive than attacks on mid-level government officials and private citizens). The study concluded that there was a 'serious risk' of intermediate terrorist incidents, including MANPADS attacks on civil airliners, and called on relevant agencies to 'investigate means of strengthening controls over terrorist acquisition of ... man-portable rocket launchers' and to 'monitor or initiate' research and design programs on devices or techniques for frustrating rocket attacks against civil aircraft...'. Even though the report was distributed by the Secretary of State, Henry Kissinger, its impact was minimal. In October 1977 – a year and a half after the report's release – the Study Group's Chairman observed that '... no formal actions were taken to implement [its] findings'.[13]

The results of the free-wheeling distribution of the new missiles and the *ad hoc* response to the terrorist threat they posed were not surprising. By the late 1970s, several terrorists and insurgent groups had acquired MANPADS. As the number of groups increased, the likelihood of a successful attack against a civil aircraft grew with it. It was only a matter of time before intelligence networks failed and the police arrived too late.

That terrible day was September 3rd, 1978.

flight 825

Air Rhodesia flight 825 had just started the routine trip from the lake resort of Kariba to Salisbury (now Harare), the capital of Rhodesia (now Zimbabwe), when its fifty-two passengers were jolted by an explosion. 'The whole plane shook', recalled passenger Anthony Hill. Those on the right of the plane watched in horror as flames poured out of the two starboard engines. The pilot, John Hood, radioed the control tower; as he prepared to crash land in rebel-infested woods, the tower crew heard him mutter 'we're going in'. They were the last words the crew would ever hear John say.

Hood deftly guided the faltering aircraft towards a cotton field. The plane touched down smoothly and, had it not been for a hidden *donga* (ditch) in the middle of the field, most of the passengers probably would have survived. Instead, the plane slammed into the ditch and cart-wheeled across the field, breaking into large, fiery pieces. Moments later, eighteen people stumbled from the wreckage, stunned by the catastrophe. Five went for help while the others huddled together, waiting for a rescue party that would arrive too late. They had not been waiting long when a group of men approached. The survivors thought they were villagers who had seen the crash and had come to help. They were wrong. The men, all armed with automatic weapons, were members of Rhodesian Patriotic Front, a Soviet-backed black nationalist movement that sought the overthrow of Rhodesia's bi-racial government. The rebels ordered the survivors to stand. Before emptying their rifles into the defenseless group, one of their executioners solemnly declared 'You have taken our land. We are going to kill you all'.[14] Three of the survivors managed to escape into the woods when the RPF opened fire. Rhodesian soldiers found the bullet-ridden bodies of the rest the next day.

Air Rhodesia initially dismissed rumors that a missile was to blame for the crash but an intense four-day investigation confirmed what many already knew: the innocents on flight 825 were the first victims of a new and terrifying threat to commercial airliners.

bleeding the soviets

the 1980s

From African refugees that smuggle handfuls of bullets in motor oil cans to state-sponsored networks that feed the voracious armament appetites of insurgent groups, the ways of trafficking small arms and light weapons are many and varied. Of the state-sponsored trafficking networks, few will ever compare to the multi-billion dollar, multi-national smuggling network that tipped the scales in favor of the Afghan rebels in their mortal struggle against the Soviets. This network is the archetypal example of government-sponsored covert arms trafficking, and an exploration of it reveals the benefits, difficulties and consequences of pursuing foreign policy goals by arming insurgent groups.

The following chapter also explores the costs and benefits of the government-to-government sales that make up the vast majority of arms transfers. Governments use arms sales to pursue many different objectives – military, diplomatic, economic and political – each of which is briefly explored through the case study of US Stinger missile sales to the Middle East in the 1980s. Also profiled is an essential element of the layered defense against the proliferation of MANPADS: legislative oversight. Imbuing the legislative branch with the ability to monitor, place conditions on and occasionally stop arms transfers is a good way of preventing ill-conceived transfers.

afghanistan and the stinger missile

The Soviets invaded Afghanistan on Christmas Eve, 1979. For the next nine years, they waged a merciless scorched earth campaign against any and all resistance. The Afghan tribesmen greeted the Soviets in the same way that their forefathers had greeted the British a century earlier – with unrelenting violence. By all accounts, the *Mujahedeen* were fearless, resourceful and brutal. Newly arrived Russian recruits were told the story of a Soviet soldier who, while patrolling an air base, came across five burlap sacks. The soldier poked at one of the bags, which oozed blood. Explosives experts were dispatched but the contents of the sacks were more terrifying than any bomb. Inside each was a Soviet soldier that the *Mujahedeen* had 'wrapped inside out in his own skin'. The story may be a legend but it conveyed an important message to the new conscripts: soldiers who surrender to the *Mujahedeen* meet grisly ends.[1]

Yet despite the fear they instilled in the Red Army, the *Mujahedeen* were poorly equipped and dying by the thousands. By 1982, make-shift hospitals in neighboring Pakistan – and graves in Afghanistan – were overflowing with the victims of the Soviet's killing machines, including the infamous Mi-24 *Hind* helicopter gunship.[2]

The Hind is a fearsome weapon. Seventeen meters long and four meters high, it is fast, nimble and bristles with weapons. The four-barrel 23 mm machine-gun that protrudes menacingly from its nose obliterates targets with the hundreds of bullets it disgorges per minute. Mounted on the helicopter's wings are 2-inch rockets and AT-2 *Swatter* anti-tank missiles, which can rip through steel fifty centimeters thick. Its grotesque appearance adds to its monster-like aura. The huge face of the Hind is distorted by the bulbous protrusions of two cockpits that resemble enormous tumors. It was the ugliest and the most loathed military aircraft used in Afghanistan.[3]

Journalists who visited wounded *Mujahedeen* in the Red Cross Hospital in Peshawar got an earful about the gunship and the rebels' desire for vengeance. 'Every time a Russian helicopter gunship strafes a village', Haji Mangal Hussain told *The New York Times* reporter Nicholas Gage, 'every man in it will not rest until he has drawn Russian Blood'.[4] What the *Mujahedeen* wanted more than anything was a way to neutralize the Hind. Their wish would be granted by an unlikely collection of patrons, the most colorful of whom was a skirt-chasing, binge-drinking, self-proclaimed 'Israeli Commando' Congressman from Lufkin, Texas.

charlie wilson and the covert arms program

Before his wildly successful campaign on behalf of the *Mujahedeen*, US Congressional Representative Charlie Wilson's most notable achievement had been keeping his Congressional seat despite his personal excesses. The Texas Republican's affinity for alcohol, extravagant junkets and beautiful women earned him the nickname 'good time Charlie' and nearly cost him his career. In 1980, for example, a night cavorting with cocaine-snorting showgirls in a Las Vegas jacuzzi led to an inconclusive but intense federal investigation that kept Wilson and his staff on edge for months.[5]

Behind these foibles was an irreverence, charisma and unshakable confidence that made Wilson the ideal champion for the besieged Afghan rebels. From Congressional field trips to Pakistan to rousing soliloquies on the House floor, Wilson had a persuasive tool for every occasion, and employed them all in his crusade for the *Mujahedeen*. One former Congressional staff member recalls attending a meeting with several *Mujahedeen* organized by Wilson. The grizzled Afghan warriors regaled their Washington audience with tales of breathtaking heroism and martyrs who doused themselves in petrol and hurled their burning bodies into Soviet trucks. The staff member was so moved by their stories that he joined Charlie's crusade, burying money for the aid program in the voluminous Defense Department funding bills.[6]

When Wilson took up the *Mujahedeen*'s cause, the size and scope of the CIA's covert aid program was relatively limited. Its goal was to kill Russian soldiers, not expel them. In the minds of its architects, an aid program capable of expelling the Soviet Union would have to be enormous – too large to remain even nominally covert – and too overt an American presence might prompt the Soviets to retaliate against Pakistan. So instead, the CIA accepted Pakistani President Zia al Haq's exhortation to 'keep the pot boiling, but not boil over': to support the *Mujahedeen* without provoking the Soviets into retaliating militarily against Pakistan.[7]

The American motivation for arming the *Mujahedeen* was both visceral – pay-back for Vietnam – and pragmatic – damaging the Soviet war machine. The CIA's Afghan station chief Howard Hart calculated that every dollar spent on the *Mujahedeen* cost the Soviets eight to ten – an excellent return on a relatively modest investment. The program also imposed an opportunity cost on the Soviets that undoubtedly appealed to the Defense Department's top brass: every soldier, helicopter, tank and fighter aircraft sent to Afghanistan to fight CIA-backed rebels was one fewer on the main Cold War battlefield – the European front.[8]

anatomy of a covert arms program

The disparate group of countries that supported the Afghan aid program had little in common other than their fear of Soviet expansion into Central Asia. Most of the money for it came from the governments of the United States and Saudi Arabia, which matched US funding dollar-for-dollar starting in 1980. Initial funding ($500,000 in 1979) was modest but grew rapidly, reaching $630 million in 1987. This money was used to buy everything a guerrilla army could need: hundreds of Japanese pick-up trucks, small arms and ammunition from Turkey and blue mules from Tennessee. The People's Republic of China – the USSR's estranged communist ally – was a steady supplier of millions of dollars' worth of mine-clearing equipment, inexpensive AK-47 assault rifles, 12.7 mm machine-guns and rocket-propelled grenades. The CIA also invested in one-time purchases from random, sometimes bizarre, sources. In 1983, they found forty million rounds of Lee-Enfield rifle ammunition stored in Yugoslavian mushroom caves. Because the mushroom growers wanted their caves back and the Yugoslav army disliked the Russians, the CIA was able to buy the ammunition for less than half the going black market rate.[9]

The CIA spent countless hours co-ordinating shipments from all over the world. Most weapons arrived in Pakistan by ship but a small percentage was flown into Islamabad. Once they reached Pakistan, the Inter-Services Intelligence Agency (ISI) – Pakistan's main intelligence organization – took over. ISI agents coordinated all training, transport and distribution of the weapons while they were on Pakistani soil. This arrangement was both advantageous and aggravating for the Americans, who benefited from the resulting 'plausible deniability' and the ISI's in-depth knowledge of all things Afghan but also gave them little say over how the weapons were distributed. Control of the billion-dollar program made the Pakistanis kingmakers, and some of the kings they made were not exactly paragons of Jeffersonian virtue. Case in point: Gulbuddin Hekmatyar. A militant Islamic fundamentalist and the ISI's favorite commander, Hekmatyar allegedly threw acid in the faces of women who did not cover themselves properly and personally executed his own men for minor infractions. At the time, however, the primary objective was to kill Russians, and radicals like Hekmatyar were killing them by the hundreds. 'We might share a few goals [with the *Mujahedeen*]', observed Islamabad Station Chief Milt Bearden, 'but only a fool would think we shared real values'.[10]

Mujahedeen commanders controlled the final leg of the distribution network, which began at the Pakistani-Afghan border and ended at the front lines. ISI Chief Mohammad Yousaf called this part of the journey the 'most complicated, chaotic and time-consuming operatio[n] of the war'. From Peshawar and Quetta, lorries carried the shipments to bases just inside the Pakistani border. There, the supplies were loaded into small trucks and onto the backs of camels, horses and mules, which inched their way along treacherous mountain passes and over dangerously exposed open areas. The slow-moving, expensive animal trains were highly vulnerable to the Hind gunships, which slaughtered them by the dozens.[11]

It was during the Afghan leg of the distribution chain that the weapons were most vulnerable to diversion. The CIA tried to minimize pilfering by monitoring the shipments and pressing the Pakistanis to punish the worst offenders. Electronic beacons were attached to some of crates and packages, which allowed the CIA to monitor them during the entire length of their journey. Others were tracked using satellite imagery. The CIA also hired Afghans to monitor the price of weapons in local arms bazaars. If prices for AK-47s plummeted soon after the *Mujahedeen* received a large rifle shipment, the CIA knew the rebels were selling the guns to local arms dealers rather than using them to kill Russians. The ISI contributed to these efforts by assigning a Major to the task full time and punishing the worst Afghan offenders by reducing their shipments. Despite these efforts, weapons continued to leak from the CIA pipeline. '[W]e do sell some of your weapons', confessed one *Mujahedeen* commander. 'We are doing it for the day when your country decides to abandon us, just as you abandoned Vietnam and everyone else you deal with'.[12]

MANPADS and the mujahedeen

Because of the havoc wrought by Soviet air power, the CIA was constantly looking for new and better anti-aircraft weapons, including MANPADS. Early in the program, they had some morale-boosting successes but just as many spectacular failures. An example of the latter was the British Blowpipe. The Americans reportedly paid $44 million for hundreds of the missiles, which former ISI Director Mohammad Yousef called a 'disaster'. In his 1992 account of the Afghan war, Yousaf recalls a battle in which thirteen Blowpipe missiles fired at exposed Soviet aircraft all missed their targets: 'a duck shoot in which the ducks won'. Soviet Strelas – which the CIA acquired from a corrupt Polish general – were only marginally more effective. Yousaf estimates that only three per cent of the missiles fired at Soviet aircraft resulted in kills. Despite the weaponry pouring into Afghanistan, Soviet aircraft continued to rule the sky, laying waste to Afghan villages and decimating the caravans that re-stocked the *Mujahedeen*'s arsenals. What the rebels needed was a quantum leap in their antiaircraft technology; a silver bullet that would allow the *Mujahedeen* to turn the tables on the dreaded Hind gun ships.[13]

enter the stinger missile

In 1985, Afghanistan was enduring its sixth year of Soviet occupation. One million Afghans had died, a million and a half had been injured and six million had been displaced. The Soviet conscripts were also suffering; more than two thousand were killed in 1984 alone. On the other side of the world, the residents of Rancho Cucamonga, California were busy assembling the delicate circuitry of the cutting edge FIM-92 Stinger missile. Many of the workers in the sprawling General Dynamics factory probably knew little about the *Mujahedeen* and their mortal struggle against the Soviets, but their product – stored in a warehouse with the motto 'if it flies, it dies' emblazoned on the wall – would soon become the crown jewel of the CIA's Afghan aid program.[14]

The idea of sending Stingers to the *Mujahedeen* had been around for some time but many senior US and Pakistani leaders still believed the risks outweighed the benefits. Such a blatant sign of US interference could prompt the Soviets to retaliate militarily against Pakistan, which would have been a significant blow to American influence in the region and an unmitigated disaster for Pakistan. Military officials also worried about technology loss. What if the Soviets captured one of the missiles? By reverse-engineering it, they could unlock many of the missile's secrets. The resulting technical insights could be used to develop counter-measures that would reduce the effectiveness of a weapon that took fifteen years to develop. Worse still, the *Mujahedeen* might sell Stingers to the Iranians who might pass them on to the anti-American terrorist organizations they supported. These and other concerns – forcefully expressed by officials at the Defense Department and the CIA – were enough to keep proponents of sending Stingers to the *Mujahedeen* at bay until early 1986, when the president of Pakistan, Zia ul-Haq, suddenly put the issue back on the table.[15]

Islamabad Station Chief Bill Piekney 'could feel his jaw dropping' when he heard Zia tell Senator Orrin Hatch – who had flown to Pakistan specifically to lobby the Pakistani President about the Stingers – that he did indeed want the missiles. For years, Zia had resisted introducing the weapon into Afghanistan, which he feared would cause the pot to bubble over. As the gate-keeper of the Afghan aid program, he held all the cards. As long as he opposed Stinger missile shipments, discussion amongst US policy-makers was academic. Conversely, his endorsement blew the door wide open. After Hatch returned to the United States and spread the word that Zia now wanted Stingers, opposition within the Reagan Administration collapsed. The President's March 1986 memo notifying Congress of his intention to ship Stingers to Afghanistan was the final nail in its coffin.[16]

congress and the stinger missile

Congressional opponents of the Stinger shipments would not be so easily mollified, however. Starting in 1982, lawmakers repeatedly locked horns with the administration over proposed Stinger sales to Middle Eastern governments. Opponents of these sales, who feared the Stingers would be used against Israel or end up in the hands of terrorists, won most of these battles. And by the time Reagan's memo on the Stinger shipments to Afghanistan landed on their desks in the spring of 1986, control advocates in Congress appeared to have the upper hand.

The battles between Congress and the Reagan administration over Stinger sales in the 1980s are important for several reasons. First, they highlight the benefits – economic, military and diplomatic – of government-to-government arms sales, and the many arguments marshaled to justify these sales. Secondly, these battles are textbook examples of the importance of Congressional (or parliamentary) oversight of arms exports, including the export of MANPADS. A strong and active legislative branch can help to tame the excesses of an overzealous executive and ensure that decisions regarding arms exports reflect the full range of national interests. At the same time, this struggle reveals the mercurial nature of the legislative process. The same Congress that fought tenaciously to block Stinger sales to governments that were hostile to Israel blithely accepted the transfer of the same missiles to Islamic guerrilla groups.

Congress's ability to scuttle the Stinger sales comes from a US law that gives legislators the power to block the largest and most sensitive arms transfers. This is the corner-stone of Congressional oversight of arms transfers which, in turn, is an essential part of America's multi-faceted defense export control system. Lawmakers must be notified in advance of arms sales over a certain value and can stop them by passing a joint resolution of disapproval. Passing such a resolution is incredibly difficult but the mere threat is often enough to prompt the State and Defense Departments to scrutinize some proposed sales more closely and to abandon others altogether. Congress also influences arms transfers by authorizing studies and holding public hearings on arms export policies, and by passing laws that prohibit or restrict arms sales to particular countries or regions. Congressional control over the budgets of the agencies that co-ordinate arms transfers is another, significant source of influence.

The opening shots in the battle between Congress and the Reagan administration over the Stinger missile transfers were fired in February 1982, when Reagan's defense secretary, Casper Weinberger, told the press he favored selling Stinger missiles and fighter planes to Jordan. Israel's parliament forcefully opposed the proposal, as did half of Congress, who went on record as opposing the sale unless Jordan entered into peace negotiations with Israel. This outcry, coupled with Jordanian resistance to joining the Middle East peace process, prompted the Administration to shelve the sale. Two years later, they tried again. On March 1, 1984 the administration formally notified Congress of its intention to sell 1,600 missiles to Jordan and 1,200 to Saudi Arabia. Congressional opponents mobilized immediately and by mid-March it was clear they had the support of most of their colleagues. Yet it was the surprisingly sharp criticism of US policy in the Middle East by Jordan's King Hussein, not Congressional opposition, that ultimately sunk the sale. On March 15, the King accused the US of 'succumbing to Israeli dictates' and playing election-year politics with its Middle East policy. Facing a hostile Congress and an ungrateful client, the Reagan administration begrudgingly withdrew the Stinger sales proposals for the second time.[17]

After two stinging rebukes from lawmakers, which embarrassed the Administration and alienated the Saudis and Jordanians, Reagan made his first, tentative attempt to circumvent Congress. In April 1984, the Administration announced that it was leasing four Stinger missile systems to the Saudi royal family for use on King Fahd's new yacht, the *Abdul Aziz*. The lease attracted little attention from lawmakers, which the President apparently interpreted as a softening of congressional opposition. In May, he again signaled his intention to sell 1,200 missiles to Saudi Arabia, and again Congress responded with an emphatic no. Facing yet another policy defeat, Reagan waived Congressional notification requirements (an action permitted under US law) and ordered an emergency shipment of two hundred launchers and four hundred missiles to Saudi Arabia.[18]

While perfectly legal, so blatant an end-run around Congress is risky, especially during an election year. Lawmakers have several ways of expressing their displeasure with a wayward administration, many of which are politically costly. This is particularly true with arms sales. Congress can cut funding for military aid programs, add burdensome conditions or reporting requirements to specific arms sales, hold embarrassing public hearings and lambaste the administration in the press. With a presidential election less than six months away, Reagan's use of the emergency waiver was politically perilous.

Why would he take such a chance? Ostensibly, it was to counter the Iranian military threat to Saudi Arabia and the oil tankers servicing the Persian Gulf. While curbing Iranian aggression in the

Gulf was a reasonable argument for *providing* Stingers, it was not a compelling argument for *selling* them. The Administration could have leased the missiles to the Saudis, thereby addressing immediate security needs while giving Congress the final say over ownership. Leasing the missiles would only have satisfied the administration's military objectives, however, and Reagan had several policy goals. Accomplishing the others required that the missiles be sold outright to the Saudis.

The Reagan Administration viewed Saudi Arabia as the 'keystone of our strategic interests in the Gulf' and providing the Kingdom with America's finest missile would show King Fahd that the Administration was willing to expend political capital to satisfy his defense needs. Leasing the Stingers would not send the same message. Furthermore, if Congress ultimately decided against the sale, the Saudis would be forced to return them, compounding their humiliation.[19]

Arms sales are also used to build long-term relationships between national defense establishments. When a country purchases a major weapons system from a foreign supplier, they're not just buying a tank or a jet fighter. They're also signing up for the years of training and the steady stream of spare parts, ammunition and upgrades needed to integrate the new weapons into their armed forces and keep them running. Policymakers often argue that this interaction translates into influence – both within the recipient's defense establishment and over their defense and foreign policies. Proving this link (if and when it exists) is always difficult. Proving it to Congressional opponents of the Stinger sales would have been next to impossible.

Not only did the Administration bypass Congress, it sent twice as many missiles as originally proposed – and sent them after the lawmakers had left town for the Memorial Day (28th May) holiday. Congress was livid. 'You have jeopardized not only the emergency authority you used in this case, but probably other emergency authority available to the administration', chided Republican Robert Kasten, Chair of the foreign affairs subcommittee of the powerful Senate Appropriations Committee. Administration officials endured similar tongue lashings from several other lawmakers, who were as incensed by Reagan's heavy-handed tactics as they were by the shipment. Ultimately, however, there was little they could do. The missiles had arrived in Saudi Arabia and getting them back would be next to impossible.[20]

Reagan had the sense to wait until after the election in November – which he won handily – before re-engaging lawmakers on the Saudi Stinger request, which was only partially filled by the emergency shipment in May. Over the next year and a half, he periodically tested the waters in Congress, discovering each time that little had changed. Finally, in March 1986, the President submitted yet another Saudi arms sales package to Congress. Instead of billions of dollars' worth of fighter jets, tanks and other big items, however, this one contained only missiles. Yet it still contained eight hundred poison pills that Israel's allies in Congress would never swallow – more Stingers.

The Administration offered several boilerplate arguments for the sale, iterations of which veteran lawmakers had heard a thousand times before. Citing 'high-level appeals' for the weapons from the Saudi government, one official warned that if the US failed to 'respond to Saudi Arabia's legitimate defensive needs at this critical point, our credibility will be seriously eroded and our message of deterrence to Iran undermined'. Implicit in this statement is the assumption that the arms package would bolster Saudi Arabia's ability to respond to Iranian aggression. But large weapons orders take years to fill and, unless the weapons are taken from existing stocks and rushed to the recipient, the immediate military impact is minimal. Administration officials admitted as much when they conceded that the first batch of missiles would not be delivered until 1989, prompting many to question just how they would help check the 'urgent' threat from Iran.[21]

The Administration also wheeled out the tried and true 'if-we-don't-sell-them-weapons-somebody-else-will' argument. Failure to fill Saudi orders, reasoned the administration, would prompt the Saudi royal family to take its business elsewhere. Fewer arms sales would mean less interaction between the Saudi officials and their US counterparts which, in turn, would mean fewer opportunities to influence Saudi defense and foreign policies. US influence in the region would suffer and the Saudis would end up with comparable, foreign weapons anyway. This is a common and, to some degree, valid argument. Because most types of weapons can be acquired from many sources and there are no universal standards for arms exports, countries denied weapons by one supplier can simply take their business elsewhere. There are exceptions; countries under UN arms embargoes have a hard time finding legal sources of weaponry, and certain weapons – or weapons of the quality and performance sought by the importing country – may only be available from one supplier. But in most cases, governments can pick and choose weaponry from several suppliers that is roughly comparable in cost, quality and performance.

Lawmakers were skeptical of the administration's arguments. 'For nearly two decades, the United States has been almost reflexively granting Saudi arms requests', fumed Representative Mel Levine. 'But our policy has neither yielded Saudi support for key United States initiatives, nor resulted in Saudi co-operation in advancing United States security interests in the Middle East.' Saudi support for the Palestinian Liberation Organization (PLO), its 'shabby treatment' of Egypt since it made peace with Israel and its cozy relationship with Libyan dictator Mohammar Qaddafi were all glaring examples of how billions of dollars in arms sales had failed to shape Saudi policies.[22]

The defense industry joined the debate on the Administration's side, drawing attention to the high-paying manufacturing jobs that would be lost as a result of America's high-mindedness. While crass and blatantly self-serving, the economic argument for arms sales is often very persuasive, especially to lawmakers with large defense plants in their home districts. To illustrate their point, industry spokesmen highlighted the economic damage caused by Congress' earlier refusal to sell advanced fighter aircraft to the Saudis, who bought British Tornado fighter jets instead. As one industry representative explained:

On programs like the F-15 [and] the Tornado, there is usually about a three-to-one ratio of follow-on training, maintenance, more spare parts, modifications and new facilities to handle the new equipment, so you're looking at another $20 billion [in lost revenue] on top of the $7 billion [cost of the planes themselves] in the next 15–20 years.[23]

Even the siren song of million-dollar defense contracts was not enough to sway a remarkably united Congress, however. On May 6, 1986 the Senate voted seventy-three to twenty-two to block the sale. The next day, the House of Representatives passed its own joint resolution of disapproval by an equally large margin. Faced with the choice of becoming the first President to have an arms sale officially blocked by Congress or modifying the missile package, Reagan opted to mollify his critics. Two weeks later, the Administration announced that it was dropping the Stinger missiles from the package.

Control advocates had prevailed again. That they preserved so broad a coalition in the face of unrelenting pressure from a popular president is truly remarkable – a tribute to the rigor of the 'checks and balances' in the US arms export system and to the importance of legislative oversight of arms sales.

congress and the afghan stingers

It was against the political backdrop of the thwarted Stinger sales to the Middle East that the Congressional battle over the Afghan Stingers took place. Leading the opponents of the Stinger shipments were Dennis Deconcini, the junior Senator from Arizona, and Les AuCoin, an eleven-year veteran of the House of Representatives from Oregon. Siding with the Administration were several Congressional heavyweights, including the senior Senator from Arizona, Barry Goldwater.

President Reagan notified Congress of his decision to send Stingers to Afghanistan in March, 1986. By the third week in April, Deconcini and AuCoin had introduced bills in both the House and the Senate opposing the Stinger transfers. AuCoin's legislation was straightforward: no Stingers for guerrillas or paramilitary forces, period. Deconcini's approach was more unorthodox. Instead of banning the shipments outright, his bill imposed the same stringent security requirements on Stinger shipments to rebel groups that applied to government recipients: a mandatory monthly count of all missiles, an annual physical inspection conducted by US military personnel, and storage facilities with 'class 5 steel vault doors secured by [a] two-key operated high security padlock' and 'a full-time guard force or combination [of] guard force and intrusion detection system'.[24]

While reasonable in the context of government-to-government transfers, where weapons are stored in accessible military depots, the requirements were unrealistic and unenforceable in Afghanistan. The Pakistanis were loath to allow any Americans into Afghanistan, let alone teams of inspectors traveling the country in search of stockpile security violations. Even if the CIA could somehow persuade the Pakistanis to co-operate, convincing the *Mujahedeen* to comply – and monitoring their compliance – would have been nearly impossible. 'The *Mujahedeen* were very independent', observed a former Pentagon official who worked on the covert aid program. Had the US tried to impose restrictions on their use of the Stingers, 'the Muj would have said "go fuck yourself"'.[25]

AuCoin's bill was sent to the Subcommittee on Arms Control, International Security and Science, where it languished until it was discarded at the end of the congressional session eight months later. Deconcini's legislation would have suffered the same fate had he not shifted gears and tried a different approach. In May 1986, he repackaged his bill as an amendment to the '*Barry Goldwater Department of Defense Reorganization Act of 1986*', which happened to be on the Senate floor at the time. Several lawmakers rose in opposition to the amendment but none offered a persuasive response to Deconcini's concerns about diversion of the missiles to terrorists. Some side-stepped the issue entirely, arguing that the proposal unduly encroached on executive branch prerogatives. Others rightly pointed out that the requirements were incompatible with 'the real world of contemporary, guerrilla-style warfare' but then failed to provide realistic alternatives for safeguarding the missiles. In the end, however, Deconcini's colleagues in the Senate, including fellow Democrats, voted over-whelmingly against him. Most lawmakers probably recognized that the amendment would have halted Stinger shipments to the *Mujahedeen*, and they were not prepared to deprive America's Holy Warriors of their silver bullet. So instead they paid lip service to the need for 'serious and searching examination' of Deconcini's con-cerns but did little – at the time or afterward – to make it happen.

Three months later (to the day), Deconcini tried again. He submitted the same proposal, packaged in the same way – as an amendment to other legislation. The same general arguments were made and the results were basically the same – sixty-three votes for and thirty-seven against. The major difference between this attempt and the one in May was time. Time had run out. Pakistani military officers had completed a stint at the US Army's multi-million dollar, state-of-the-art Stinger training facility and soon they would be passing on their newly acquired skills to *Mujahedeen* Stinger teams. If they had not arrived already, planes carrying the first batch of the two thousand Stingers destined for the Holy Warriors would soon be landing in Pakistan. The trans-fer was, for all practical purposes, a *fait accompli*.[26]

The irony could not have been more striking. The same Congress that had repeatedly bloodied the nose of one of America's most popular presidents to prevent Arab governments from acquiring Stingers blithely stood by while hundreds of the same missiles were sent to Islamic guerrillas, some of whom were also hostile to Israel but less accountable than the Saudi or Jordanian governments.

The CIA did its best to control the Stingers. It kept meticulous records of the missiles exported to Afghanistan, required the *Mujahedeen* to turn in a spent missile tube for every new missile they received and expanded its network of Afghan spies to moni-tor the rebels' use of the missiles.[27] But once the Stingers left US shores, anything could happen to them. Just thirteen years after US officials indignantly lectured their Soviet counterparts on the dangers of uncontrolled MANPADS, the American government let loose two thousand of its own. US MANPADS control efforts had reached their nadir.

the 'stinger effect' in afghanistan

In his account of the Afghan war, former ISI chief Mohammad Yousaf provides the following description of the Stinger's electrifying debut in Afghanistan:

> When the leading Hinds were only about 600 feet from the ground [Commander] Ghaffar yelled 'Fire' and the Mujahideen's shouts of 'Allah o Akbar' rose up with the missiles. Of the three, one malfunctioned and fell, without exploding, a few meters from the firer. The other two slammed into their targets. Both helicopters fell like stones to the airstrip, bursting into flames on impact ... Two more missiles were fired, with another success and a near miss with a helicopter that had landed. I believe one or two others were damaged due to heavy landings as the frantic pilots sought to touch down in precipitate haste. Five missiles, three kills – the Mujahideen were jubilant. Their cameraman was so overcome with elation that he tried to film while running around, so his record of the event consisted largely of blurred images of sky, bushes and stony ground. He only steadied himself sufficiently to film the black smoke pouring from the wrecks ...[28]

Rarely has the nay saying of skeptics been more thoroughly rebuked by history than in the case of the Afghan Stingers. 'If a terrorist should capture a Stinger and a manual, he's not going to be an effective Stinger gunner', observed defense analyst David Isby. 'They are not a simple weapon, and require an eighteen-step process to fire it. I suspect that Joe Afghan won't be very good at it either'. But Joe Afghan was good at it. He was so good at it that dozens of Soviet aircraft fell from the sky, boosting the moral of the *Mujahedeen* and 'send[ing] a shockwave through the Soviet air force'.[29]

As the *Mujahedeen* celebrated, the Soviets panicked. They shut down the Jalalabad air field for a month and ordered their beleaguered troops to establish ten-mile wide 'bandit free' zones around airbases. They also ordered pilots to fly higher and to fire their weapons from their maximum range, reducing their effectiveness and earning airmen the contempt of their counter-parts on the ground, who derisively referred to them as 'Cosmonauts'. Flare-dispensing helicopters began accompanying transport planes and commercial airliners departing from Afghan air fields.[30]

These measures did little to mitigate the Stinger's effectiveness. While the 'cosmonauts' sought the security of the heavens, some Hind gunners aborted missions as soon as they saw the contrail of a surface-to-air missile. The resulting disruptions to the Soviet counter-insurgency air campaign allowed more of the pack animal caravans – and their precious loads of supplies and ammunition – to survive the treacherous journey. Less tangible but just as important was the psychological element of the 'Stinger effect'. Each Hind that fell from the sky emboldened the *Mujahedeen* and sapped the moral of the Soviet soldiers and their leaders. 'After years of being unable to strike back effectively at the enemy in the air' observed Yousaf, 'the *Mujahedeen* had at last received a weapon worthy of their spirit'.[31] The 'Stinger effect' persisted despite the Red Army's best efforts. A year after Engineer Ghaffar surprised the Hind pilots near Jalalabad, the US State Department reported that '[Soviet] efforts to devise countermeasures have yet to reduce the anti air threat'. Slowly, the Soviets adjusted to the Stinger, but the *Mujahedeen* continued to shoot down aircraft (albeit less frequently). By the time the Soviets left Afghanistan in 1989, the *Mujahedeen* had used the Stinger to shoot down an esti-mated 269 aircraft.[32]

After four long years, Charlie Wilson got his silver bullet, his Hind killer. By any measure, the Stinger missile, and the Afghan aid program more generally, was an unqualified military and geo-strategic success – a testimony to the asymmetrical power of covert arms programs and the man-portable guided missiles that came of age with the Stinger. Yet the characteristics that made the missiles such a threat to Soviet military aircraft – stealth, accuracy, lethality – also made them a threat to commercial air-liners. With the withdrawal of the Soviet Union from Afghanistan two years later, the *Mujahedeen*'s silver bullets would become dangerous liabilities.

the proliferation and control of MANPADS in the 1990s

When you cannot fight your foe on the battlefield, you will hit his embassies. If they are hidden behind concrete walls, you will hit his banks. If they are protected by bullet-proof glass and armored plating, you will hit his schools, his hospitals, his resort hotels, his commercial airliners. And if the terrorists cannot board a US airliner with box-cutters, they may be able to target it with surface-to-air missiles.

Mark Thompson (Correspondent for *TIME*)

On February 15, 1989, Lt General Boris Gromov – the last Soviet soldier in Afghanistan – turned his back on the Soviet Union's 'Vietnam' and crossed the Termez Bridge into Uzbekistan. The Soviet occupation was over. The *Mujahedeen*, with the help of their international benefactors, had defeated the second most powerful military in the world. Charlie Wilson and the other 'true believers' had been vindicated. The pot had not boiled over, the *Mujahedeen* had mastered the sophisticated weapons provided by the CIA and the Soviets had buckled under the unrelenting pressure of a ragtag collection of Afghan rebels and the weight of their own bankrupt political system.

Yet the victory over the Soviets was tainted by the *Mujahedeen*'s appalling post-war behavior. After the Soviet withdrawal in 1989 and the collapse of the Afghan Communist regime three years later, America's erstwhile allies turned on each other and their own people. *Mujahedeen* commanders laid waste to the areas that they conquered, mowing down soldiers and civilians alike. Adding insult to injury, two prominent *Mujahedeen* leaders, Gulbuddin Hekmatyar and Abdul Rasul Sayaf, publicly thumbed their noses at the US during the first Gulf War, issuing statements of support for Iraqi leader Saddam Hussein.

Another worrying loose end was the disappearance of hundreds of the Stinger missiles that had been distributed to the *Mujahedeen*. The characteristics that made the Stingers so effective against the small, nimble Soviet jets and helicopters – aircraft designed to evade and neutralize anti-aircraft missiles – made them an even greater threat to the lumbering, defenseless commercial jets that had, over the previous three decades, become a favorite target of terrorists. Having reduced hijackings and bombings through rigorous airport security measures, some aviation security experts worried that terrorists would turn to weapons against which commercial airliners were defenseless.

The following chapter traces the proliferation, use and control of Stingers and other MANPADS from the late 1980s through the 1990s. The ways in which these missiles enter and circulate on the black market are explored, as are the deadly purposes for which they are used. From depriving needy populations of life-saving humanitarian aid to assassinating national leaders, the misuse of these missiles has had widespread, profound consequences. Several control strategies are also profiled, including buyback programs, undercover investigations, stockpile security, use control devices and multilateral agreements.

the stingers scatter

Charlie Wilson was not the only one vindicated by history. Senator Dennis Deconcini's fears that the *Mujahedeen*'s Stinger missiles would be acquired by America's enemies also came to fruition, and quickly. In early 1987, just months after the *Mujahedeen*'s first fateful encounter with Hind gunships, Soviet *Spetsnaz* (special forces) seized two Stinger launchers and four missiles from a group of *Mujahedeen* whom they caught napping near Kandahar.[1]

A few months later, a *Mujahedeen* Stinger team operating in one of Afghanistan's western provinces encountered an impassable river near the Iranian border. Disregarding Pakistani orders not to enter Iran, the team crossed the border and was intercepted by a group of Iranian *Passadars*, or border scouts. The Iranians confiscated their four launchers and sixteen missiles. The Pakistanis and their Afghan allies tried for months to convince the Iranians to return the missiles but to no avail.

News of the seizure surfaced in the international press in September 1987 but not until Stinger missile parts were discovered on an Iranian patrol boat did the US media take notice. American helicopters disabled the patrol boat after coming under fire from its crew during one of many altercations between Iranian and American forces during the Iran-Iraq War. Four days later, the Iranian Ambassador to the United Nations confirmed that his government had Stingers and warned that his people 'would ... use all the means we have to defend ourselves' against the US military, even America's own missiles. Deconcini blasted the administration for not heeding his earlier warnings: 'Now one of our worst enemies may have one of our best weapons in one of the most volatile regions of the world'.[2]

Over the next decade, dozens of Stingers would end up in the arsenals of insurgents, terrorists and governments hostile to the United States. Iran, Qatar and possibly North Korea and China illicitly acquired Afghan Stingers, as did Chechen separatists, Algerian fundamentalists, Kurdish rebels in Turkey and the

Liberation Tigers of *Tamil Eelam*, a brutal Sri Lankan insurgent group. The Taliban inherited dozens of them from allied *Mujahedeen* commanders and Osama bin Laden's bodyguards reportedly had access to several.[3] The 'Terrorists' Delight' was now, indisputably, in the hands of terrorists.

As bad as the Stinger problem was, it paled in comparison to the massive proliferation of Soviet MANPADS. 'There are as many Soviet-made portable missiles on the black markets all over the world as there is dirt', proclaimed one Russian analyst. Hundreds ended up in the hands of terrorists and insurgents. In 1987, French authorities seized 150 tons of Libyan weapons, including twenty SA-7 missiles, from the cargo hold of a Panamanian-flagged trawler, the *Eskund*. The shipment was one of several assembled by the Libyan government for the Irish Republican Army, which ultimately received over 120 tons of weaponry from Libya, including twelve SA-7s. Other missiles were pilfered, one or two at a time, from military arsenals. Since the early 1990s, there have been several alleged thefts of MANPADS by Russian soldiers, including an incident in 1993 when two sailors from Russia's Baltic Fleet were arrested while attempting to sell an SA-7 missile for $40,000. Trafficking in SA series missiles was so widespread that, by the late 1990s, they were in the arsenals of eleven of the fourteen non-state groups known to possess MANPADS.[4]

buying back the stingers

As American fears of Soviet world domination began to fade, other concerns came to the fore, including the terrorist threat posed by the unused Afghan Stingers. Early ideas for retrieving the loose missiles, including barter arrangements for agricultural equipment or medical supplies, were quickly discarded. The 'weapons in exchange for development' approach has worked in some cases, but post-Soviet Afghanistan would not have been one of them. With the war against the Soviet-backed Communist regime still raging, few government officials thought the *Mujahedeen* would trade in their Hind-killers for tractors.[5]

A less naïve but equally flawed proposal was to exchange the missiles for other weapons. The proposal was based on the assumption that '[o]nce the various factions fall to squabbling among themselves ... machine-guns are going to be much more important determinants of political power than Stingers'.[6] This approach incorrectly assumed that the value of the Stinger to the *Mujahedeen* was based solely on their military utility. But the rebels valued the Stinger for many reasons, and machine guns were no substitute for their silver bullet. Such an exchange would also be morally distasteful, particularly after the Communist government fell in 1992 and the *Mujahedeen* turned on each other. Eventually, the CIA settled on a third option: cash – buckets and buckets of cash. Dollars are easy to transport, widely accepted and less morally repugnant than swapping weapons that *will* be used to kill innocent Afghans for weapons that *might* be used to kill passengers on western airliners.

Weapons collection programs are a popular and at times effective strategy for mopping up black market weapons and educating people about their dangers. Yet many of these programs, particularly those aimed at collecting firearms, have little impact on the quantity or ill-effects of the illegal weaponry. Much of the difficulty stems from the ubiquity and utility of illegal firearms, particularly in the areas most in need of weapons reduction programs. War zones are often saturated with tens of thousands of small arms, which are valued as a source of protection against, and a means of exploiting, the lawlessness that pervades these environments. As a result, the demand for firearms in post-conflict and crime-ridden areas is often higher than the demand for the inducements – agricultural equipment, job training and cash – offered as part of weapons collection programs.

In contrast, the number of MANPADS at loose in a given region rarely exceeds a few dozen, and their usefulness (to anyone other than insurgents facing attacking government aircraft or terrorists targeting commercial airliners) is limited. As a result, missile buy-back programs can be very effective. In 2003, for example, US operatives persuaded Somali warlord Hussein Aideed to sell them forty-one SA-7 missiles that he had received from Eritrea in 1998. Eritrea had given Aideed the missiles in response to Ethiopian threats to bomb Eritrean-backed rebels operating from Somalia under Aideed's protection. The missiles lost their usefulness when Aideed signed a truce with the Ethiopian government a year later. No longer facing an enemy with an air force, Aideed traded the missiles for dollars. Had the US not intervened, it is possible that Aideed would have dumped the missiles on the black market instead.[7]

Retrieving the Stingers from the *Mujahedeen* would be more difficult, and policymakers familiar with Afghanistan and the *Mujahedeen* were skeptical of the Stinger recovery program from the start. 'It's prudent for the Administration to try to recover the Stingers, but I personally doubt it will succeed' observed Charlie Wilson. 'There's nothing worth as much as a Stinger and the *Mujahedeen* aren't stupid.'[8]

Wilson was right.

operation MIAS

The US and its allies started buying back the *Mujahedeen*'s Stinger missiles in 1990. The top secret program, Operation *Missing in Action Stingers* (MIAS), was administered by the Near East Division of the CIA's Directorate of Operations – the same division that had distributed the missiles in the first place. The division called upon the countries that had helped to arm the *Mujahedeen*, including Pakistan, Saudi Arabia and several European nations, to help track down the missing missiles. It was not a hard sell. 'Every western intelligence service is trying to help out because all of our governments are dead scared one of those things is going to end up in the wrong hands', observed one European military attaché. The Saudi Royal family reportedly sent aides as far as Somalia to collect wayward missiles.[9]

According to journalist Steve Coll, the CIA subcontracted much of the day-to-day work to Afghan commanders and the ISI, who received a commission for each missile they purchased on the CIA's behalf. Missiles retrieved through this program were brought to Islamabad in a small Cessna turboprop plane. There they were loaded on to intercontinental transport planes and flown to the United States for destruction by the Army.[10]

The program worked well enough to burn through its initial $10 million allocation but not well enough to retrieve all of the missing Stingers. By 1993, individual missiles were fetching $100,000 or more as CIA middlemen competed with other interested parties, including Iranian and North Korean agents. Congress responded by allocating an additional $55 million for the program, but dozens, possibly hundreds of the missiles, escaped the CIA's dragnet. According to US government officials interviewed by Steve Coll, roughly six hundred of the Afghan Stingers were still at large as of 1996.[11]

The seemingly simple task of buying back the Stinger missiles was, in practice, anything but. For a variety of reasons, the Afghan commanders were extremely reluctant to part with the missiles. Their reluctance, and the myriad other problems that plagued Operation MIAS, illustrate the difficulty of implementing even the most straightforward small arms control strategy.

Until President Najibullah's (Soviet-backed) regime collapsed in 1992, the *Mujahedeen* still had a compelling military justification for keeping the missiles. Najibullah's air force had functioning Soviet aircraft and no weapon had a better track record against those aircraft than the Stinger. 'We will not return the Stingers', proclaimed a spokesman for *Mujahedeen* commander Yunis Khalis, 'We ourselves need them most ... Does the Afghan Air Force not have aircraft?' Yet there was more to this missile hoarding than military considerations. Other forces – psychological, social and cultural – were also at play.

Stingers became an indicator of the owner's standing and access to resources. During the Soviet occupation, '[Stingers] were a sign that the "big boss" in the US liked you', recalls a former Defense Department official who worked on weapons development for the *Mujahedeen*. The more the 'big boss' and its Pakistani surrogates liked you, the more weapons and aid you received and, in turn, the more resources you had to firm up alliances and foil adversaries. These thoughts were echoed in the comments of the

Mujahedeen. 'Stingers now sell for $50,000 to $70,000 but most commanders still don't sell them because you lose prestige if you get rid of them for money', asserted Afghan commander Abdul Haq. 'The missiles are an enormous status symbol'.[12]

Cultural forces also contributed to the *Mujahedeen*'s unwillingness to part with their Stingers. As explained by former ISI chief Mohammad Yousaf, who worked closely with the *Mujahedeen* for many years, '... weapons have always played an important part in an Afghan's life. The more modern the rifle that a man owns, the higher his standing'. This phenomenon is not uncommon in weapons collection programs. A 'best practices' guide compiled by the Bonn International Centre for Conversion advises practitioners to consider this phenomenon when designing such programs. 'Males are often attracted to owning and displaying weapons even if they have no need or intention of using them', reads the guide. 'Traditional and modern cultures alike often consider the bearing of arms as a sign of honor, valor, virility or prestige'. Having leveled the playing field against the dreaded Hind gunships, the Stinger became the ultimate symbol of honor, valor, virility and prestige in Afghanistan.[13]

The *Mujahedeen*'s reluctance to give up the Stingers was not the only problem confronting the CIA. Attracted by the large payouts, con artists sold counterfeit missiles to unsuspecting middlemen, and others took advantage of the CIA's short-lived attempt to avoid transport hassles by paying for photographs of destroyed missiles instead of the missiles themselves. The arrangement was abandoned when the CIA started receiving what it suspected were multiple photos (for multiple payouts) of the same dismantled missile.[14]

More disturbing than the money lost to fraud was the money doled out for real missiles. Anxious to prevent terrorists from acquiring their deadly Stingers, the Americans 'delivered boxes of money to the warlords who were destroying Afghanistan's cities and towns'.[15] No example better illustrates this dilemma than the CIA's 1997 attempt to buy back the Taliban's Stinger stockpile. By that time, the fundamentalist group's track record of brutality and oppression was well-established. In February 1996, *The New York Times* ran a front-page article describing how the Taliban had 'plunged millions of Afghans into a new chapter of brutality that echoes the harshness of Afghanistan's distant past' through the subjugation of women, a medieval penal system and the categorical rejection of western learning and technology. Money paid to the Taliban would undoubtedly be used to strengthen and expand their brutal rule.[16]

But CIA Station Chief Gary Schroen's job was not to weigh the relative ethical merits of funding warlords versus protecting civilian airliners. His job was to retrieve the Stingers, and Schroen believed that the Taliban might be willing to part with their missiles for a quick infusion of cash. The station chief met Taliban leader Mullah Omar's chief aide in Kabul in February, 1997. After politely listening to Schroen's pitch, the aide declined his offer. 'We are keeping these Stingers because we're going to use them on the Iranians', he reportedly told Schroen. Had the Taliban agreed to surrender their Stingers, they probably would have demanded the prevailing black market rate of around $100,000 per missile which, if they sold their entire estimated stockpile of fifty-three missiles, would have added $5 million to Taliban war chests.[17]

Operation MIAS also provided Gulbuddin Hekmatyar with yet another opportunity to publicly defy his former benefactors. During a press conference in Tehran in August 1993, he declared '[t]he Afghan government does not intend to allow even a round of ammunition to be taken out of Afghanistan'.[18] Hekmatyar's insolence – broadcast to the world – was yet another reminder of the transient nature of alliances between governments and insurgent groups, and the difficulty of retrieving their weapons when these alliances end.

evaluating operation MIAS

Press coverage of Operations MIAS was almost uniformly negative. Citing US and Pakistani officials, the *Washington Post* reported in 1994 that the program 'has been plagued by failures, miscalculations and wasted money ...'. Specific failures identified in the article included low recovery rates and soaring black market prices, which it blamed on poor record-keeping and 'haphazard [recovery] efforts' by the CIA. The author also pointed to a bungled recovery operation in which Pakistani paramilitaries seized three Stingers from Mullah Abdul Salam, an Afghan commander whose love of modern weapons earned him the nickname 'Rocketi'. Rocketi had just agreed to sell the missiles back to the CIA when, unbeknownst to the Americans, the Pakistanis decided to take the missiles by force instead. During the raid, one of Rocketi's brothers was killed and another arrested. Outraged, Rocketi – who was also known as the 'kidnapping king of Afghanistan' – took several Chinese and Pakistani hostages, demanding $225,000 in cash, the return of the three Stingers and his brother's release for their safe turn. The Pakistanis refused and the hostages languished in Rocketi's makeshift prison until a combination of threats and offers to release his brother convinced Rocketi to free his captives. In July 1994, the hostages – bedraggled by a year of malnutrition and beatings – were released.[19]

Despite instances like Rocketi's kidnapping spree, it is unfair to blame the CIA for the failure to recover all the missiles. Even under ideal circumstances, exported light weapons are difficult to track, and conditions in Afghanistan were far from ideal. Once the missiles were distributed to the *Mujahedeen* commanders, the Americans – who were generally prohibited from entering Afghanistan – had to depend on paid Afghan informants and the Pakistanis for information on their whereabouts. The decentralized and perpetually shifting battle front, coupled with Afghanistan's rugged terrain, made it impossible to track every Stinger, even for fellow Afghans.

Even the US military, with its legions of administrators and logisticians, has had trouble keeping track of its Stingers. In 1994, the General Accounting Office (GAO) – Congress's investigative arm – studied the Army's compliance with accounting and handling requirements for the approximately six thousand Stingers sent to the Gulf during the 1991 war with Iraq. The GAO found that the Army tracked the missiles *en route* but once they reached Kuwait, inventory and stockpile security procedures broke down. '[A]t the entry point' reads the GAO report, 'combat units took what they wanted ... some missiles were transported unguarded on trucks driven by third country nationals, and some ammunition sites were left wide open'. One Army official recalled 'a load of Stinger missiles [that] was found unguarded on the side of a road'. Reflecting on the lack of accountability, another official concluded '... it would be "pure luck" if none of the missiles were lost'. Upon returning to the United States, the Army had trouble accounting for all of its missiles. It claimed to have 6,373 Stingers in its inventory – the same number that had been shipped to the Gulf – but could not reconcile its physical holdings by serial number. According to the GAO report, '[a] comparison of serial numbers showed that forty of the missiles sent to the Gulf were not returned to the depot, other Army locations, or the other services'. Three years later, the Army still did not know where those missiles were.[20]

Even if the CIA had somehow managed to do what the US Army could not and track every missile, they still would have faced the *Mujahedeen*'s reluctance to give back the missiles. As explained above, the CIA's 'carrot' – huge cash payouts – only worked some of the time, and they had no 'sticks' to use when they failed. There was no military aid to suspend (the Bush administration cut off all aid to the *Mujahedeen* in January 1992), and Rocketi's kidnapping spree underscored the folly of trying to retrieve the missiles by force.[21]

The power to address the threat posed by the proliferation of the Afghan Stingers lay not with the CIA but with the US military. Had the Defense Department developed and installed use control devices in the missiles prior to shipping them to Afghanistan, Operation MIAS might not have been necessary.

controllable enabling

Use control devices – and particularly *controllable enablers* – are a promising but largely neglected nonproliferation tool. The controllable enabler, which is similar to the technology used in anti-theft devices for car radios, is incorporated into the circuitry of the missile's guidance system. When the operator turns on the missile system, it searches for an enabling code. If the code has been entered, the missile functions normally. If the code has not been entered or if it has expired, the missile will not operate at all. Advocates are quick to point out that the enabler would not require the user to punch in a code in the heat of battle; the missile could be enabled well in advance of any encounters with enemy aircraft and remain enabled for as long as necessary.[22]

In theory at least, the controllable enabler would significantly reduce the threat posed by lost or stolen missiles. Stolen missiles that had not been enabled – presumably the majority of a country's holdings – would be of little use. Enabled missiles would still pose a threat but for a much shorter time (only the length of time for which they are enabled). The device would also reduce black market demand. Terrorist and insurgents are unlikely to seek out weapons that may suddenly stop working just before a carefully planned attack or when government planes are bearing down on them. Similarly, few arms traffickers would invest tens of thousands of dollars in merchandise that may be useless a week later.

Some experts believe the technology would also be relatively inexpensive. Robert Sherman, former Director of the Advanced Projects Office at the US Arms Control and Disarmament Agency, estimates that design costs would be minimal (under a million dollars) and installation costs at the time of manufacture would be 'immeasurably small'. Fitting existing missiles with enablers would be more costly and difficult but would still be possible.[23]

But enablers were not available in the 1980s and still aren't available today. Repeated requests from Congress and other government agencies to develop and install the devices went unheeded by the Pentagon, which reportedly objected to the cost of updating enabling codes and the possible adverse effects the enablers could have on missile performance. In 1986, Congress appropriated $1 million to study the feasibility of developing use control devices for Stingers. A year later, lawmakers called for an additional $4 million to develop the 'Stinger System Safeguard' and berated the Army for 'not assign[ing] sufficient priority to this effort in the past'. The next year, similar language and additional money was included in the FY1989 Defense Appropriations Bill, but to little apparent effect; shoulder-fired missiles continued to be manufactured and exported without use control devices.[24] The US military was not alone. None of the major MANPADS producers equipped their missiles with use-control devices.

Without enablers (or comparable technology), the US government's ability to control the Stingers shipped to Afghanistan was extremely limited. Gary Schroen and his team did the best they could with the resources they had but the odds were against them.

The hunt for the Afghan Stingers continues to this day.

stinger stings

Long before Schroen and his team started chasing MANPADS in Afghanistan, their domestic counterparts were chasing MANPADS traffickers in the United States. Domestic law enforcement, and particularly undercover operations (stings), are an essential component of any control strategy. Local and national investigators work with informants, prosecutors, and military officials to catch arms traffickers ranging from first-time amateurs to seasoned veterans. These investigations often last for years, span several countries, involve hundreds of recorded phone calls and, occasionally, staged 'sales' of real (but inert) missiles. Like the criminal networks that seek out these missiles, the investigations are often international. Since the early 1990s, American investigators have worked with their counterparts in Russia, China, Germany, Britain, and several other countries to arrest would-be missile traffickers.

Ideally, these operations not only take individual arms traffickers off the street but also have a chilling effect on the rest of the criminal underworld. Less confident in their ability to distinguish real clients from undercover agents, traffickers are likely to be wary of doing business in countries where stings are common, less willing to deal with new clients and reluctant to traffic in the weapons that attract the most attention from authorities. Supply sources dry up, black market prices rise to compensate for the decrease in supply and the increased risk and, consequently, criminals are forced either to look elsewhere for their weapons or – ideally – abandon their search altogether. This is the ideal scenario. How closely this scenario corresponds with reality is a matter of debate.

The first highly publicized 'Stinger sting' in the United States began in March and culminated in the arrest of Kevin Gilday, an arms dealer with a history of weapon sales to Middle Eastern and Eastern Bloc clients. US Customs officials claim that Gilday agreed to help deliver a 'laundry list' of arms and dual-use technology to a laundry list of America's enemies: sophisticated computers to East Germany, C130H transport planes to Libya, aircraft tracking systems to Syria and, most disturbing, firearms, Stinger missiles and anti-tank missiles to the Irish Republican Army and Iran. Investigators corresponded with Gilday more than a hundred times over the course of the eight-month investigation, during which he revealed his master plan.

Gilday and his three accomplices were not newcomers to the world of arms trafficking. They owned front companies in several countries, had contacts in the governments of several client states and with the Irish Republican Army (which had contacts in additional governments) and were familiar with the arms export rules and regulations of the countries in which they operated. Since the items they intended to export were controlled (that is, required an export license) and the recipients were either terrorist organizations or countries under arms embargoes, they needed documentation that created the appearance of a legal sale. Gilday's British cohort was to provide this documentation: letters of credit, purchase orders, contracts and fake end-user certificates that falsely identified the governments of Brazil and Saudi Arabia – both acceptable end-users – as the recipients. Everything was in place when, on November 25, 1986, the scheme came to an abrupt end. Gilday was arrested in Washington, DC, near the Capitol building and a year later, he was tried and sentenced to several years in prison.[25]

Not every sting nabs a sophisticated arms dealer. Less than six months after Gilday was convicted, US officials learned of another attempt to arm the Iranians, but one of a very different nature. On January 15, 1988, Customs agents arrested a father-son team for attempting to purchase components for Iran's *Hawk* Air Defense Systems. During the investigation, the son also expressed an interest in buying 'unlimited quantities' of Stinger missiles. That the team was not the *crème de la crème* of the criminal underworld was apparent right from the start. Instead of seeking a back-channel source for the missile components, the son simply picked up the phone and called the manufacturer, Raytheon – a large, established defense firm that routinely works closely with law enforcement agencies. During what was presumably his first conversation with a Raytheon executive, the son revealed that he was seeking Hawk missile components for his father's *Iranian* import/export company and that he intended to ship the components via a third country. The executive claims that the son even offered him a $100,000 bribe to obtain the necessary paperwork.

The phone call not only reveals the son's complete ignorance of industry practice but also an utter lack of common sense. By the late 1980s, American producers of weapons sought by Iran were reporting all requests for sensitive components to the US Customs Service. A competent arms trafficker would have known that anything he said to the Raytheon executive could be reported to Customs investigators. Recognizing that the would-be arms traffickers were either 'extremely naïve or extremely stupid' and posed no real threat, Judge Mark Wolf took pity on them. He sentenced the father to an additional four months in jail (he had already served ten) and his son to six months (the time he had already served), and five hundred hours of community service.[26]

In January 1990, the FBI arrested two more bumbling Stinger seekers, this time in South Florida. Seamus Moley and Kevin McKinley also did not fit the Hollywood arms dealer stereotype. The two Irishmen lived quietly in one of the ubiquitous West Palm Beach trailer parks, attracting little attention except when they locked themselves out of their trailer, which happened frequently. They spent their evenings mixing with the locals at a nearby bar, the *Chateau*, where they met a gun enthusiast named

Michael Burdof. When Moley and McKinley learned of Burdof's hobby, they started pestering him about a bolt-action .50 caliber sniper rifle that they had seen in a magazine. Burdof tolerated the persistent Irishmen until they told him that they wanted the gun to kill British troops in Northern Ireland. Then he called the FBI.

Investigators acted quickly, setting up a meeting with Moley and Mckinley the next evening. They met at *Big Daddy's Lounge* – the antithesis of the penthouse suites and private yachts where arms traffickers do business in the movies. With the working class rhythms of *ZZ Top* and *Lynyrd Skynyrd* setting the mood, under-cover agents established a rapport with the Irishmen, who talked freely about .50 caliber sniper rifles and killing Brits. They expressed no interest in Stinger missiles until the undercover agents brought them up at a meeting in December. A month later, however, the duo had collected $47,500, the price of one missile, which they deposited in a safety deposit box set up in the name of one of the undercover agents. Later that day, a third conspirator, Joseph McColgan, drove to a West Palm Beach warehouse to pick up the Stinger. FBI agents reported that when they handed McColgan the missile, he tried to cram it into his suitcase. When that didn't work, he tossed it into the front seat of his car and started to drive away. The agents arrested him moments later.

The next day, McColgan played dumb. 'I'm just a poor Irishman here on holiday and I was entrapped by certain people here', he told the press. His lawyer must have made a persuasive case to this effect because at least one juror believed him, saying: 'It's a shame that the government spends tons of money to entrap these three guys who really weren't looking for any trouble'. Nonetheless, the judge's decision to rule out entrapment as a defense paved the way for a guilty verdict, which was delivered on December 11, 1990. Six months later, the defendants were sentenced to four years in prison.[27]

These cases raise questions about the competence of the traffickers caught by law enforcement officials and the threat they actually pose. The young Iranian was incapable of acquiring *components* for lesser weapons, let alone one of America's most heavily guarded missiles. Moley and his cohorts had more experience but it is hard to imagine a scenario that ends with them walking away with a working Stinger. Gilday and his team were better positioned to acquire and deliver the Stingers but their interest in them was fleeting. Are law enforcement agencies only catching the least competent and committed traffickers? If so, could the resources used to catch and prosecute them be put to better use?

It is probably true that sophisticated arms traffickers look elsewhere for MANPADS. US government regulations for storing and transporting Stingers are among the most rigorous in the world, and most arms traffickers probably seek out softer targets. Stingers are stored in bullet-, fire- and theft-proof magazines that are continuously monitored by Intrusion Detection Systems or armed guards. The magazines are surrounded by two-meter high fencing and each gate is monitored by a security camera. Vehicles entering and leaving the facilities are subject to random searches, some four thousand of which were conducted at US Army installations during the first half of 1994 alone. To prevent theft by employees, the serial numbers on each Stinger are recorded and missile counts are taken at the end of each shift. Access to storage room keys is limited and two-person locks are used to ensure accountability. Exhaustive monthly, semi-annual and annual physical inventories are taken. Physical security and stockpile management requirements for private defense contractors are also rigorous.[28]

Yet implementation of this system has been far from perfect, underscoring the importance of complementary control strategies, such as stings. In 1994, the General Accounting Office visited seventy-eight of the Army's shoulder-fired missile storage sites. At eighteen locations, inventory records were off by as many as 142 missiles. The GAO also found broken alarm systems, missiles stored on flatbed trucks, missing fencing and sub-standard magazine locks. At some sites, security guards searched unfamiliar vehicles but waved through those they recognized.

The potential threat posed by such security lapses was underscored in 1992 by an anonymous phone tip received by the Dallas office of the Bureau of Alcohol, Tobacco and Firearms. The informant told the ATF that nine Stinger missiles at the nearby Red River Army Depot had been moved to an insecure area in preparation for unauthorized removal from the depot. The caller also claimed that twenty missiles had already been stolen in this manner. The Bureau immediately contacted the Army, which dispatched investigators to the depot. The Defense Department later reported that 'the Army Criminal Investigative Division found no evidence of criminal activity. A one hundred percent inventory of Stinger missiles at the depot was conducted, and all missiles were accounted for'. They glossed over one rather chilling detail, however. The nine missiles supposedly being staged for theft were exactly where the informant had said they would be.[29]

Thus, even in countries with the resources and the will to keep a close eye on their weapons, relying solely on stockpile security is a mistake. Alarm systems fail, regulations are violated and even the best hiring practices cannot weed out every corruptible employee. Preventing theft and diversion requires a multi-layered defense – and undercover operations are a crucial layer, even if many of the traffickers thwarted are only second-class criminals. Even seasoned traffickers slip up and a strong, well-funded law enforcement network should be in place to catch them when they do. For Italian investigators, such a moment came in August 2000, when a complaint from an unpaid prostitute led to the arrest of arms trafficker Leonid Minin. Had Italian law been different, their heads-up police work might have permanently shut down the operations of one of Africa's most infamous merchants of death.[30] Furthermore, although lesser traffickers may not get anywhere near a working Stinger, they may have the skill to acquire other dangerous items. Seamus Moley, for example, reportedly man-aged to procure 2,900 explosive detonators from a US source and ship them to his comrades in Ireland. The detonators were used in a wave of bombings that rocked Northern Ireland in 1992.[31] Moley's Stinger conviction took him off the streets, preventing similar shipments.

triggering genocide

Despite the best efforts of law enforcement and other government agencies around the world, hundreds of MANPADS ended up in the arsenals of thuggish regimes, terrorists and insurgents. During the 1990s, these missiles were used to threaten military aircraft, hinder humanitarian aid operations, and trigger mass slaughter. Of the fourteen aircraft lost by the US Air Force during the 1991 Gulf War, four were shot down by Russian *Needles* (SA-16s). The British also lost several jets to these missiles. The lumbering transport planes used by aid agencies are also vulnerable to MANPADS, which are widely proliferated across areas most in need of aid. In the autumn of 1990, millions of East Africans facing starvation were deprived of food aid when the Sudanese government barred relief agencies from flying into refugee centres. The government's stock of SA-7 missiles forced relief agencies to heed the order.[32]

The most devastating MANPADS attack of the decade took place in the tiny, strife-torn central African country of Rwanda in 1994. Tension between the Hutu majority and the Tutsi minority had been growing as Rwanda's president, Juvenal Habyarimana, prepared to end the civil war with the Rwandan Patriotic Front, a powerful Tutsi insurgent group. During the peace negotiations, extremist Hutus spewed genocidal hatred from their radio stations while stockpiling weapons and compiling 'hit lists' of Tutsis and moderate Hutus. By April 1994, Rwanda was a tinderbox.

The spark that ignited it came from Habyarimana's presidential jet, which crashed as it was preparing to land at Kanombe military airport near Kigali. The resulting chaos provided the pretext for extremist Hutus to begin their long-awaited genocide against the Tutsis, whom they referred to as 'cockroaches'. The rest of the story is well known. During a hundred-day orgy of violence, Hutu militias slaughtered 800,000 Tutsis and moderate Hutus while the rest of the world did nothing.

Ten years later, the circumstances surrounding Hamyarimana's death are still unclear. It is widely believed that assassins positioned near Kigali airport brought down the presidential jet with two SA series missiles. According to the *Sunday Times*, Russian officials were able to trace the serial numbers of the missiles to two Soviet SA-16s sold to Uganda. The identities of the assassins and how they acquired the missiles remain mysteries, however.[33]

Blaming the Rwandan genocide on the proliferation of MANPADS is like blaming World War I on the bullet that killed Archduke Franz Ferdinand. The missile attack was a proximate, not an ultimate, cause, and there is little reason to think that, had the missiles missed their target, another catalytic event would not have produced the same tragic results. Yet Habyarimana's murder – and the hell that it unleashed – is a terrible reminder of just how vulnerable a nation's leaders (and thus an entire nation) can be to modern light weaponry. There are other ways to bring down presidential planes but the range, accuracy, ease of use and availability of man-portable missiles makes such attacks easier and therefore more likely to succeed.

Despite incidents like the shooting down of President Habyarimana's jet, the MANPADS threat remained a peripheral issue. A 1993 conference, sponsored by the US Federal Aviation Administration, examined the proliferation of MANPADS mainly as a long-term threat requiring further study rather than as an immediate threat requiring immediate action. For most policymakers, the MANPADS threat was still largely an abstraction – 'a dangerous thing on the periphery', in the words of former State Department official, Herb Calhoun.[34]

The mysterious crash of Trans World Airlines flight 800 temporarily thrust the MANPADS threat back into the spotlight. On July 17, 1996, the Paris-bound plane exploded just off the coast of Long Island, New York, killing all 230 people on board. For months afterwards, the American press was filled with speculation about possible causes, which included shoulder-fired missiles. Investigators downplayed the likelihood of this explanation,[35] but the specter of a MANPADS attack lingered.

The Clinton Administration responded to the crash by setting up a high-profile *Commission on Aviation Security and Terrorism*, chaired by Vice President Al Gore. The Commission was nothing new. Over the years, several study groups had examined the terrorist threat to commercial aviation, including the MANPADS threat. What distinguished the Gore Commission from its predecessors was the catalytic effect it had on the State Department. Secretary of State Madeline Albright embraced the Commission's call for decisive action against the MANPADS threat and, three years later, her team unveiled *Elements for Export Controls of Man-Portable Air Defense Systems* – the first international agreement on MANPADS export controls.

the wassenaar arrangement

The Wassenaar Arrangement (WA) is an international institution that promotes transparency and responsibility in the transfer of conventional arms and dual-use items. Member states – which include many of the major arms exporters – agree to establish export controls for specific weapons (control lists) and share information on arms transfers to non-member states. Through these (voluntary) requirements, the WA helps harmonize and improve control lists and increase awareness of potentially destabilizing (or otherwise problematic) arms sales. The WA is also a forum for developing guidelines and procedures that reflect the 'best practices' of individual countries. It was in this capacity that the Wassenaar Arrangement became the springboard for *the Elements for Export Controls of Man-Portable Air Defense Systems.*

The *Elements* were the product of two years of patient, behind-the-scenes cajoling by American negotiators, who faced varying degrees of opposition from several key WA members. Some states feared that the *Elements* would pave the way for similar agreements, each of which would further constrain their arms export programs. Others objected to the singling out of MANPADS for special treatment, or dreaded the prospect of another round of arm-twisting by the interfering Americans.[36] As a result, negotiations on the *Elements* were 'touch and go' recalls Joe Smaldone, a member of the American delegation. Just as one country would come on board, another would backslide. A round of meetings and phone calls would follow, and the waffling delegation would drop its objections. This back-and-forth continued for weeks until, slowly, the dissenters started to come around. The pieces were falling into place but not fast enough; on the eve of the December 2000 plenary session, the Russian delegation was still sitting on the fence. Luckily, the *Elements* weren't scheduled for discussion until the afternoon session of the second day (December 1), giving the US delegation thirty-six hours to win over the Russians and address any last-minute objections from other delegations. The Americans met with members of the Russian delegation on the sidelines of the November 30 plenary session and hammered out a compromise on the draft text. The next day, the US team assembled for an early morning meeting, ready to brief interested delegations on the draft agreement's contents and address last minute concerns. Nobody came. 'This caused some degree of uncertainty' claims Smaldone, 'but was soon used to [our] advantage'.

Later that morning, the US delegation informed the plenary session that it interpreted the low turnout for the morning meeting as tacit approval of the draft text. 'That smoked out the Korean delegation', recalls Smaldone. The Koreans' concerns were relatively minor and the Americans were able to address them during a coffee break. Not all the delegations were so easily placated, however. Just hours before the fateful afternoon plenary, the US team met with the Ukrainian delegates, who said that they had 'serious problems' with the draft text and wanted the *Elements* to be considered merely as 'recommendations'. The US insisted that the *Elements* had to be binding to be meaningful, and persuasively explained how potential implementation problems identified by the Ukrainians could be overcome.

Victory was in sight. One more meeting with the Russians and the Ukrainians was all that stood between WA delegates and the first multilateral agreement on MANPADS exports. Not only did the Russians co-operate but 'were instrumental in getting the Ukrainians to agree to the final text', Smaldone claims. The rest of the day was just a formality. After the US delegation informed the plenary that agreement on the *Elements* had been reached, the Chairman proposed that the *Elements* be adopted by the Plenary. Hearing no objections, he announced it agreed.

As the lead US negotiator was wrapping up business, he ran into the head of the Russian delegation. The American expressed his deep appreciation for his co-operation. With a hint of good-natured sarcasm, the Russian replied 'Go tell Madeline Albright she got her Christmas present'.

The *Elements* were an unequivocal step forward. Member states had agreed to a long list of eligibility criteria, export controls and stockpile security and information sharing requirements, including taking into account the adequacy of the recipients' physical security arrangements and their general ability to protect against loss, theft and unauthorized transfers before approving a MANPADS export; storing missiles and launchers in separate locations; transferring MANPADS only to other governments; seeking the consent of the supplier before re-transferring imported MANPADS; and promptly informing the supplier of theft, loss or diversion of MANPADS missiles, launchers or component parts.

How big a step forward is a matter of debate, however. If widely and fully implemented, the *Elements* would certainly help to reduce the illicit trade in MANPADS. Strong export criteria, and especially a ban on transfers to non-state groups, would reduce future transfers to likely proliferators and instances of diversion. Storage and inventory requirements would make theft more difficult, as would the requirement to bring together missiles and launchers only for immediate military purposes.

Yet achieving universal implementation of any international agreement is tricky, let alone a politically binding agreement negotiated in a forum that has no monitoring and enforcement mechanism. The small WA Secretariat has little power over participating states. It lacks the mandate and the infrastructure to monitor implementation and if it were to discover a violation, it has no way of punishing the violator. The secretariat cannot impose economic sanctions, expel member states or issue reprimands. Other member states can 'name and shame' violators but the onus is on the states themselves to identify, document and punish such violations.

The other significant limitation of the *Elements* is the Wassenaar Arrangement's limited membership. Only thirty-four of the dozens of countries that have produced or imported MANPADS are bound by it. China, Iran, Pakistan, Egypt, and North Korea – all manufacturers of MANPADS – are not WA members. One possible solution is to convince them to join the Wassenaar Arrangement, which is open to any country that meets four basic requirements: that they produce and export arms or industrial equipment, align their national control lists with the WA control lists, fully maintain effective export controls and adhere to the policies and guidelines of eight major non-proliferation regimes.[37] But meeting these requirements is difficult for many countries and some, such as North Korea, are so far outside the non-proliferation fold that membership in the Wassenaar Arrangement is inconceivable. For these reasons, the *Elements* – and multilateral agreements in general – are an important but inherently limited part of the layered defense needed to address the MANPADS threat.

the post-mombasa scramble

Today is a time for reflection, and tomorrow must be better than yesterday.

Premnathsing 'Dev' Jokhoo
Assistant Superintendent, Mauritius Police Force
SALW Topical Seminar, Kampala, October 2004

Most of the 261 passengers on Arkia Airlines flight 582 had no idea that they had come under attack. Shortly after taking off from Moi International Airport (Mombasa, Kenya) on November 28, 2002, they felt a slight bump, which was followed by immediate assurances from the flight crew that the disturbance was just a 'technical mishap'. Only after they entered Israeli airspace several hours later did they learn the truth: their plane had come within a few feet of being the first civilian MANPADS casualty outside of a conflict zone. 'It's [my] first time to Kenya. And my last', declared one passenger, Shali Harbi.[1]

Within days, investigators found the errant missiles in a corn-field about six miles from the launch site. Their serial numbers linked them to a batch manufactured by the Soviets in 1978. Investigators also found the launchers, which were reportedly produced by a Bulgarian company in 1993 and sold to Yemen in

1994. According to UN investigators, the missiles were smuggled from Somalia into Kenya by sea in August 2002. How they ended up in Somalia, and ultimately in possession of east African affiliates of al Qaeda is unknown, at least outside of government intelligence circles.[2]

The failed attack was the most significant MANPADS event since the assassination of Rwanda's president in 1994. It shattered the notion that only pilots flying over war zones need worry about the missiles. The notion itself was unfounded, but the fact that terrorists and insurgents had generally refrained from attacking planes outside of conflict areas provided false comfort to policymakers, most of whom were not ready to confront the MANPADS threat head-on. The Mombasa attack took away that crutch.

The following chapter examines the global counter-MANPADS campaign catalyzed by the Mombasa attack and the difficulties of implementing it. Several control measures not covered in previous chapters, such as technical counter-measures (anti-missile systems) and destruction assistance programs, are explored. The chapter also takes a closer look at the terrorist threat to commercial and military aircraft – which has received unprecedented attention since the incident in Mombasa – and the proliferation threat posed by excessive weapons stockpiles.

the US responds

Overnight, the event in Kenya elevated the proliferation of MANPADS from policy side note to 'one of the greatest threats to commercial aviation'.[3] The American government's response was infused with an urgency that, for once, matched its rhetoric. Two weeks after the attack, the US Homeland Security and National Security Councils convened an inter-agency task force to 'develop an aggressive plan to assess and counter the MANPADS threat'. The resulting strategy – which reflected the input of twenty-one different US government agencies – called for action on three broad fronts: proliferation control and threat reduction, tactical measures and recovery and technical counter-measures.

Within months of the first task force meeting, dozens of US government officials were actively implementing this strategy. In March 2003, the Transportation Security Administration completed a preliminary vulnerability map of major US airports, several of which were ordered to make 'major security improvements', including round-the-clock security patrols and 'tightened electronic surveillance of the flight paths'. US officials conducted similar evaluations at several airports in foreign cities, including Athens, Istanbul, Manila, Baghdad and Basra. The State Department spearheaded negotiations on several multilateral MANPADS agreements and intensified efforts to locate and destroy missiles in insecure foreign stockpiles. Public education campaigns, international buy-back programs and changes to accounting procedures for exported Stingers were also initiated.[4]

The effect of the attack on Congress was just as profound. In early 2003, the House of Representatives held its first closed hearing on the MANPADS threat in years. If the goal was to scare Congress into action, the hearing was successful. At a press conference several weeks later, Congressman John Mica, chairman of the House Aviation Subcommittee, revealed just how profoundly the testimony had affected him:

> I went into the meeting somewhat skeptical of, one, the threat; and two, whether we had the ability to deal in a technological fashion with the threat ... I came out convinced that this is probably one of the most serious challenges that we face ... I don't lose sleep over many things that I deal with and I've dealt with a lot since September 11th, but I can tell you since that hearing I have lost some sleep ...[5]

Mica was not alone. Two months earlier, Representative Steve Israel and Senator Barbara Boxer introduced the *Commercial Airline Missile Defense Act*, which called for the installation of anti-missile systems on all turbojet aircraft used by air carriers by the end of 2003 – a multibillion dollar undertaking. The bill didn't pass, but other legislation quickly followed. By the end of the 108th Congress two years later, lawmakers had introduced some fourteen pieces of legislation addressing the MANPADS threat.

the world responds

Mombasa galvanized the rest of the international community as well, prompting dozens of national, regional and international initiatives. Israel was first out of the blocks. In December, the Israeli foreign ministry began a world-wide push to limit MANPADS sales to state sponsors of terrorism, conduct a worldwide MANPADS inventory and improve controls in several problematic countries.[6] Since then, *El Al* airlines has reportedly installed the Flightguard flare system on all its aircraft, making it the first airline in the world to equip its entire fleet with anti-missile systems. Russia also took up the Counter-MANPADS mantle, pushing through a transparency agreement in the Commonwealth of Independent States (CIS). The agreement, *Measures to Control the International Transfer of* Igla *and* Strela *Man-portable Air Defense Systems by Member States of the Commonwealth of Independent States*, commits all CIS members (except Turkmenistan, which refused to join) to keep records of MANPADS exports, share this data with other CIS members and designate a point of contact to co-ordinate MANPADS data requests. It also facilitates criminal investigations and other law enforcement activities by requiring states to compile a list of contacts that law enforcement officials in other countries can call on when they need information about a particular exported missile.

In recent years, Russia has also strengthened its national controls on MANPADS. Most notably, it now includes end-use monitoring conditions in contracts for missile sales to other countries. The conditions oblige receiving states to allow Russian experts to conduct on-site inspections of exported missiles. The government is also speeding up the process by which decommissioned missiles are destroyed, collaborating more closely with foreign intelligence and law enforcement officials to thwart traffickers, and is reportedly exploring possible launch control devices for its missiles.[7]

Dozens of other countries have contributed to the burgeoning global effort by endorsing the steady stream of multilateral initiatives spurred by the Mombasa attack. By the third anniversary, five regional organizations had adopted MANPADS control guidelines – a remarkable achievement given the glacial pace at which such agreements are usually negotiated. In June 2003, the G8 adopted an 'Action Plan on Transportation Security and Control of MANPADS'. Six months later, the Wassenaar Arrangement strengthened its *Elements*, which were also adopted by the Organization for Security and Cooperation in Europe in May 2004, the Asia-Pacific Economic Cooperation Forum in November 2004 and the Organization of American States in June 2005.

These agreements build on the MANPADS control guidelines laid out in the WA's original *Elements*, adding new obligations and fleshing out existing ones. The requirement in the expanded *Elements* to include launch control features in newly designed missiles is particularly important. As explained in Chapter 6, use control devices are – at least in theory – a very promising way of reducing both the supply of and demand for black market MANPADS. Also noteworthy are the provisions requiring recipient governments to provide continuous (24-hour) surveillance of storage sites and to limit access to teams of at least two authorized personnel, both of which are important for preventing internal theft. Finally, these agreements bring additional countries into the fold, including China, a major producer and exporter.

Several countries have already taken concrete steps to implement these agreements. At least two members of the Wassenaar Arrangement have strengthened their national laws and regulations on MANPADS.[8] Similarly, members of APEC agreed to evaluate at least one of their airports for vulnerability to MANPADS attacks by 2006.[9] Yet many of the constraints that hindered the Wassenaar Arrangement's original *Elements* also affect these agreements. They lack monitoring and enforcement mechanisms, relying instead on individual member states to detect and punish violations. Furthermore, many countries that possess MANPADS are not parties to any of these agreements. Since even a few stray missiles pose a grave threat to commercial airliners, extending these standards and practices to every country, regardless of the size of their stockpiles or their status as non-producers, is essential.[10]

The International Civil Aviation Association (ICAO) and the United Nations are attempting to address this problem by universalizing existing agreements. In 2004, ICAO passed a resolution urging its 189 member states to apply the principles defined in the *Elements*. A similar resolution adopted by the United Nations General Assembly calls on members to support international MANPADS control efforts. While these resolutions help to further important norms, they suffer from the same monitoring and enforcement limitations as the international agreements they attempt to buttress.

iraqi missiles unleashed

Just as international efforts to rein in the proliferation of MANPADS were gearing up, Operation *Iraqi Freedom* dealt them a tremendous blow. On March 20, 2003 a multi-national coalition led by the United States invaded Iraq with the goal of deposing the country's dictator of twenty-five years, Saddam Hussein. The outmatched Iraqi military put up little resistance and, three weeks later, Baghdad fell. As the regime collapsed, so did any semblance of control over the hundreds of arms caches scattered throughout the country. Suddenly, one million tons of weaponry was fair game. Looters swarmed over the caches, carting away thousands of weapons, including MANPADS.

Iraq is a troubling reminder of the threat posed by indiscriminate arms exports to militaristic regimes and the sudden, violent removal of these regimes. During the Iran-Iraq war (1980–1988), arms-producing states sold an estimated $61 billion worth of weapons to Saddam Hussein. So many weapons flowed into Hussein's arsenals that, on the eve of the Iraqi invasion of Kuwait in 1990, Iraq had the fourth largest military in the world. The subsequent UN arms embargo and war to liberate Kuwait significantly reduced Iraq's military might but did not stop the weapons stockpiling. The Iraqi government continued to buy weapons on the gray and black markets and to produce some itself, including assault rifles, heavy machine-guns, rocket-propelled grenades and mortars.[11] By the time coalition troops marched into Baghdad, Iraq was one big weapons depot.

The US military took important, but inadequate, steps to collect and dispose of this weaponry. American troops and Iraqi contractors started destroying some as early as April 2003 and by late October, ordnance disposal teams were destroying an estimated hundred tons of weapons every day. Six months after the end of major combat operations, however, many weapons depots were still dangerously vulnerable to looters. Journalists privy to the depots have written hair-raising accounts of their lethal treasures and the inability of over-stretched coalition forces to secure them. *The New York Times* correspondent Raymond Bonner visited a site about forty miles from Baghdad:

> ... not a soldier or a guard was to be seen ... missiles are everywhere ... there is a 30-foot missile with Russian markings, still on its trolley ... Two *Exocet* missiles ... lie on the ground several hundred yards away. They seem to have been rendered largely useless by the bombing, but parts may be of some value ... Outside in the rubble was a shoulder-fired SA-7, a Russian-made surface-to-air missile, caked with dirt.[12]

Recognizing the unique threat posed by the MANPADS pilfered from these caches, the US Army set up a buy-back program which, despite bewilderingly low pay-outs of $500 or less (a fraction of the going rate for MANPADS on the international black market), netted hundreds of missiles. In October 2003, US troops manning a weapons collection site in Northern Iraq were approached by an Iraqi in a pick-up truck. The Iraqi turned in two missiles, collected the pay-out and drove away. Later he returned with nearly *200 missiles.* 'I think he wanted to find out if we really were going to pay. When we did, he went back and returned with the others', recalled one of the soldiers. Before he left, the Iraqi promised to return the next day with forty more missiles.[13]

But many of the four thousand MANPADS estimated to have been in Iraqi arsenals before the war remain unaccounted for. Occasionally they resurface, either in weapons caches seized by coalition forces or in the hands of insurgents, who use them to shoot down coalition aircraft. The deadliest missile attack occurred in November 2003, when an SA-7 hit the rear of a transport helicopter ferrying soldiers to Baghdad International Airport. Sixteen of the soldiers died and twenty were wounded. Since then, insurgents have shot down several other aircraft, including a DHL cargo plane similar in size to a commercial airliner.

The post-war pillaging of Iraq's mammoth arms depots illustrates the need for restraint in the international arms trade. Excess accumulation of weaponry by aggressive regimes not only upsets regional military balances and prolongs conflicts, it also poses an acute proliferation threat. By filling Iraq's massive weapons orders, arms exporters (inadvertently) contributed to the tripling of the number of MANPADS on the black market when the regime fell. Weapons buy-back programs have recovered some of the missiles but recovery efforts are never totally successful, and hundreds, possibly thousands, of Saddam's MANPADS are still missing.[14]

a technical solution?

There may be a technical solution (or partial solution) to the MANPADS threat. Anti-missile systems have been used for years on military, Head of State and some corporate planes, with good results. These systems, often referred to as 'technical countermeasures' use high-tech gadgetry to confuse, blind, or destroy missiles after they are launched. They are the last line of defense against a MANPADS attack and, as such, are potentially important elements of national MANPADS control strategies.

Yet, like other control measures, anti-missile systems are not perfect. Widespread commercial use of these systems would be an experiment, and equipping the entire global fleet of commercial airliners (or hundreds of airports worldwide) would be cost prohibitive and would take years, possibly decades. Even if this were possible, many systems only protect against certain types of

MANPADS and could be overwhelmed by a large salvo of missiles fired simultaneously. Further complicating this equation is the possible evolution of MANPADS technology. The use of anti-missile systems for military purposes provides a strategic incentive for MANPADS-producing states to develop missiles capable of overcoming these systems.

These issues make decisions about anti-missile systems difficult for policymakers, who must weigh the costs and benefits of protecting their airliners from MANPADS (still only a theoretical threat in most countries), evaluate the technical merits of different anti-missile systems and – should they decide to equip airliners with the systems – find the money to pay for their installation and maintenance.

billion dollar questions

In October 2003, the US Department of Homeland Security (DHS) launched a multi-million dollar, multi-phase program for the evaluation of anti-missile systems, focusing primarily on adapting existing military systems for commercial use. Depending on what DHS ultimately recommends, American policymakers will face some tough choices. Their decisions will have far-reaching implications not only for their constituents but also for other governments, many of which are also contemplating anti-missile systems for their country's airliners. Below is a brief overview of the three main policy options:

option #1: do nothing

This has been the world's approach to airliners and anti-missile systems for three decades, and most countries have not lost a single airliner to a MANPADS attack. The obvious advantage of this option is that it would save the airlines and governments billions of dollars – resources that could be used to address more established (less hypothetical) security threats. Simply because terrorists have not engaged in a particular type of attack doesn't mean they can't or won't, however. The last thirty years are replete with examples of non-state groups successfully acquiring and using MANPADS: thirty-five commercial aircraft have been hit, resulting in twenty-four crashes and five hundred casualties. Most of these attacks occurred in conflict zones but the barriers to smuggling a few missiles and a few trained operators into other areas are hardly insurmountable.

If terrorists were to stage a successful MANPADS attack against a major airline, the human and economic costs would be severe. How severe is a matter of debate. Some analysts believe it would be financially devastating, particularly if several aircraft were shot down over several days. This viewpoint is pithily summarized by defense analyst John Pike: 'If they [terrorists] shot down one aircraft on one day, two aircraft on the second day, and three aircraft on the third day, how many would they shoot down on the fourth day? None, because no one would get on an aircraft'.[15] The RAND Corporation, a government-sponsored think tank, puts the price tag of a successful MANPADS attack on an American commercial airliner at between $1.4 billion (if airports are shut down for one day) and $70.7 billion (if they are shut down for a month).[16]

option #2: equip commercial aircraft with anti-missile systems

There are two primary types of anti-missile systems for planes: *flare systems* and *laser jammers*. Flare systems dispense a stream of heat-producing material to overwhelm or deceive the missile's heat-seeker. Older systems dispense pyrotechnic flares, which burn at extremely high temperatures and dazzle the missile's seeker. These systems are effective against older missiles, which chase the hottest object in the sky, but are less effective against newer missiles, which are able to distinguish between flares and aircraft. Newer flare systems use materials that generate heat signatures closer to that of the aircraft, making them more effective.[17] Laser jammers direct a laser beam into the infra-red seeker of the approaching missile, generating a target signal that is stronger than the one generated by the aircraft. The false target information fools the missile's guidance system into thinking it is off course and it responds by adjusting the missile's flight path toward the false target and away from the aircraft. The laser beam is directed at the missile until it is so off course that it no longer poses a threat.[18]

The big drawback of plane-mounted anti-missile systems is their cost. In 2004, RAND concluded that it would cost around $11 billion to install jammers on the 6,800 US commercial aircraft. Operating and support costs would add another $2.1 billion a year – about half the money currently spent on transportation security in the United States. One way to reduce the cost is to buy fewer systems and rotate them around the US commercial fleet. Northrop Grumman claims that its *Guardian* system can be removed from one plane and installed on another in less than an hour. Planes flying at-risk routes would all carry jammers, while the remaining systems would be shared by the rest of the fleet. The obvious danger of this strategy is that terrorists might be able to determine which planes are not protected, or play the odds and get lucky. This danger could be mitigated by studying (through simulations) where missiles are most likely to hit different types of aircraft, and the resulting damage to that aircraft. Planes most vulnerable to a catastrophic MANPADS attack could carry laser jammers, while other planes could be equipped with less expensive counter-measures.[19]

The other problem with flares and laser jammers is that they do not protect against every type of MANPADS; command line-of-sight (CLOS) and laser beam riding missiles are impervious to both systems. Some analysts downplay the threat posed by these missiles, pointing out that they have not proliferated widely and require more training to use effectively than infra-red seeking missiles, 'the basic operation [of which] can be taught in less than 10 minutes or gleaned from a manual'.[20] It would be foolish to dismiss the threat posed by these systems entirely, however. Many terrorist organizations are innovative, resourceful and willing to commit time and resources to teaching their members how to operate weapon systems. In the late 1970s, a defector from the Irish Republican Army revealed they were learning Russian so they could read the operating manuals of their Soviet MANPADS. Similarly, Al Qaeda has produced training films that provide step-by-step instructions on how to fire SA series missiles.

Training members in the use of radio-controlled and laser beam rider systems might be more difficult but it is hardly inconceivable. Terrorist organizations could, for example, recruit operators from militaries that employ these systems. In this regard, Iran is particularly worrying, given its history of terrorist sponsorship, its enmity toward the West and its military's combat experience with the RBS-70. During the Iran-Iraq War, Iran illicitly acquired around two hundred RBS-70 missiles, which it used against Iraqi aircraft. The members of the Iranian military who trained on and used these systems may still be around, and may be susceptible to the financial rewards or ideological arguments offered by terrorist organizations.[21]

Acquiring these systems would certainly be more difficult than their infra-red seeking cousins but it would not be impossible. Radio-controlled and beam riding missiles have been sold to over two dozen countries, including some with poor non-proliferation records. Pakistan – the epicenter of the largest nuclear smuggling ring in history – has imported hundreds of RBS-70 laser beam rider missiles from Sweden. The Pakistani government's failure to control its most dangerous weapons technology raises troubling questions about its ability to control the rest. Furthermore, even countries with decent non-proliferation track records occasionally fall prey to arms traffickers, as evidenced by the diversion of Swedish missiles to Iran.

That said, the vast majority of the MANPADS on the black market and in the hands of terrorists are infra-red seekers, and laser jammers may indeed be the most cost effective, time-tested and readily available anti-missile technology. Should policymakers decide to go with laser jammers, however, other MANPADS control efforts will become that much more important.

option #3: equip airports with anti-missile systems

Another option is to protect airports rather than individual airplanes. A technology touted for this role by the RAND

Corporation is the Mobile Tactical High Energy Laser – a chemical laser that destroys missiles in flight. Another is Raytheon's *Vigilant Eagle* system, which uses microwaves to interfere with the missile's guidance system.

The big advantage of these systems over laser jammers and flares is that, in theory at least, they protect against a broader array of threats. Raytheon claims its *Vigilant Eagle* system works against all three types of MANPADS – infra-red seekers, CLOS and beam riders. High Energy Lasers would be effective against these systems and also artillery, unmanned aerial vehicles and some cruise missiles.[22]

There are several potential drawbacks to ground-based countermeasures, however. Most significantly, they do not protect airline passengers beyond the protected airport, whereas plane-mounted systems travel with the passengers. Addressing this shortcoming would require equipping airports worldwide with ground-based systems – a daunting task. Wealthy countries would have to be persuaded to purchase and maintain the systems, and to subsidize their acquisition and maintenance by financially challenged governments. As with other anti-missile systems, ground-based counter-measures would have to be supplemented by other, rigorously implemented control strategies.

stockpile destruction

The only foolproof way of preventing terrorists and criminals from acquiring a missile is to destroy it. The obvious limitation of this strategy is that MANPADS have legitimate military purposes and most countries are therefore protective of their stocks. Some governments, however, have surplus or obsolete MANPADS that they are willing to part with, and programs that help these governments to safely dispose of surplus weapons and secure the rest are a crucial part of any effective counter-MANPADS campaign.

Some of these programs are co-ordinated through international institutions, such as the North Atlantic Treaty Organization (NATO). Through the *Partnership for Peace* program, NATO members have funded the destruction of over a thousand missiles in the Ukraine and Kazakhstan. Other programs are funded and coordinated by individual governments, the largest of which are the US stockpile security and destruction assistance programs. With little fanfare and on shoestring budgets, small teams in the State Department's *Office of Weapons Removal and Abatement* and the Pentagon's *Defense Threat Reduction Agency* have facilitated the destruction of nearly one million surplus small arms and improved stockpile security in more than two dozen countries. They are arguably the most cost effective non-proliferation programs run by the US government, and their contributions to MANPADS control efforts have been invaluable; since 2001, the State Department has funded the destruction of over 18,500 surplus and poorly secured MANPADS and the Defense Department has helped secure hundreds more.

Officials who work on these programs have seen it all: storage rooms so stuffed with weapons that rifles spill into the hallway when the door is opened, mortar rounds bursting out of rotting crates, etc. Such practices are so common that, for veterans of these programs, they are no longer noteworthy. Occasionally, however, even they are taken aback by what they find.

A 2003 trip to Liberia provided many such moments. The corrupt and brutal regime of Charles Taylor had just been deposed, and the State Department feared that the hundreds of tons of weapons that remained would be pilfered. In November, a small team went to Monrovia to assess how the State Department could support UN efforts to dispose of the weapons.

When they arrived in the war-ravaged capital, the Americans found a cornucopia of weapons from around the world. 'It was crazy', recalls one member of the team, 'there were RPGs [rocket-propelled grenades] from seven or eight countries'. Rumor had it that the combatants had also imported dozens of SA series missiles, weapons of particular concern to the Americans. When asked about these rumors, the UN officials who had inventoried the weapons caches said that they had not encountered any MANPADS. These claims were quickly belied by the discovery of two SA-7s in an ammunition cache in the former President's compound. The State Department team asked the teenagers standing guard (remnants of Charles Taylor's Anti-Terrorism Unit) if they knew of any others. The teenagers led the Americans to a locked room in the same compound, containing thirty-eight SA-7 and SA-14 systems. Apparently, UN officials had mistaken the MAN-PADS for anti-tank missiles, and had placed them in the rooms for safe-keeping. 'They were the least secured MANPADS I had ever seen', marveled the State Department official. The Americans notified the UN of their discovery and broke the seekers of the missiles, rendering them useless.[23] A trip the next day to the house of a high-ranking official in Taylor's government provided more hair-raising surprises. Inside a shed located near the house, they found two SA-7s and two SA-14s 'guarded only by a chicken with no tail feathers'.[24]

bilateral agreements: nicaragua and the US

Few destruction initiatives are as exciting and immediately gratifying as the trip to Liberia. Most involve months of tedious negotiations and are in constant danger of being derailed by unrelated political developments. The recent row over the destruction of Nicaragua's MANPADS is a good example.

As explained in Chapter 1, the Soviets flooded Central America with weapons, and the Sandinista government in Nicaragua was one of the biggest recipients, receiving, among other weapons, approximately two thousand Russian MANPADS. The superpower proxy wars in Central America eventually ended, but many of the weapons remain – attractive targets for arms traffickers.

The threat from Nicaragua's surplus stockpiles was underscored in 2001, when an Israeli arms broker operating out of Guatemala duped the Nicaraguan military into selling him three thousand AK-47 assault rifles and two and a half million rounds of ammunition. The broker claimed that the weapons were destined for the Panamanian National Police, providing a fraudulent end-user certificate as proof. Anxious to dispose of the rifles, the Nicaraguans approved the sale without taking even basic steps to check the authenticity of the certificate; a simple phone call to the

Panamanian government could have exposed the fraud. On November 2, 2001, the weapons were loaded into the cargo hull of the *Otterloo* – the only vessel registered to a Panamanian shipping company set up six months earlier. Five days later, the *Otterloo* arrived in Turbo, Colombia where the weapons were delivered to the real clients – the United Self-Defense Forces of Colombia, a paramilitary group on America's list of international terrorist organizations.[25]

It is not surprising, therefore, that the US government viewed Nicaragua's enormous stockpile of Russian MANPADS with deep concern. In February 2003, President Bush raised the issue with President Bolanos, who reportedly promised to destroy all of them as part of a broader arms reduction initiative in Central America. Despite grumbling by the Nicaraguan military, the two governments quickly fleshed out plans for the destruction program, which began in May 2003 with the disposal of 333 missiles. Two additional batches were destroyed in August and November, but trouble was brewing in the National Assembly. Members of the politically influential Sandinista party – America's Cold War nemesis – started echoing the military's call for $80 million in compensation and reciprocal reductions in their neighbors' arsenals. The US balked at the request; participants in the State Department's destruction program normally don't receive compensation, let alone $80 million. When Bolanos announced that he would destroy the rest of the missiles without compensation, the Sandinistas pounced. Their allies in the National Assembly passed a Weapons Control Law that required the President to get the Assembly's permission before authorizing the destruction or sale of the country's weapons, effectively ending the program.[26]

The situation went from bad to worse after Nicaraguan authorities arrested an air conditioning repairman who tried to sell an SA-7 missile to undercover agents. The Nicaraguan military quickly checked their stocks and reported that the seized missile was not one of theirs, which prompted public speculation by unnamed US officials that the missile was part of a 'secret stash' held by elements of the Nicaraguan military. The Nicaraguans were irate. The military called the claim 'stupid' and accused the United States of staging the sting to weaken the Sandinista party. Three weeks later, the National Assembly voted to over-ride President Bolanos's veto of the Weapons Control Law.[27]

The US responded by sending a delegation to Nicaragua, which returned with a commitment from the Nicaraguans to destroy all but four hundred of their missiles and to provide more information on the rest. The promises were not enough to placate the White House, which suspended $2.3 million in military aid, conditioning its restoration on the destruction of the rest of the missile. The sanctions had little effect. Six months passed and the Nicaraguan President was no closer to convincing the Assembly to destroy the missiles. In fact, Bolanos himself introduced legislation that authorized the destruction of only 651 missiles – four hundred short of their entire inventory – and imposed no deadline for doing so. Finally, the Bush administration relented. In October, the Administration announced that it was restoring the suspended military aid, saying only that they had 'been assured that the existing missiles are being maintained in a secure manner ...'.[28]

The diplomatic battle over Nicaragua's MANPADS is significant for several reasons. First, it underscores the importance – and cost effectiveness – of stockpile security and destruction assistance as a control measure. Destroying a thousand inadequately secured missiles cost American taxpayers just $300,000 – a remarkable bargain considering that these missiles will never, under any circumstances, end up in the hands of terrorists or insurgents. Another $200,000 – budgetary pocket change for the US government – funded physical security and stockpile management improvements that reduce the likelihood of the remaining missiles finding their way into terrorists' hands.[29]

This case also illustrates a time-tested maxim of diplomacy: arms control in any form is fragile. Governments are extremely sensitive to issues of sovereignty and national defense, and even the slightest perceived impingement can generate a storm of protest. This is particularly true when the source of impingement is the regional hegemon. Finally, this case reveals just how far up the hierarchy of US policy that MANPADS control has climbed. The March 2005 decision to suspend military aid to Nicaragua was the first time that the United States cut aid to an ally over concerns about small arms proliferation. And not just any ally but a member of their embattled 'Coalition of the Willing' – the countries that provided troops and other support to the United States' internationally unpopular war in Iraq. The fact that the administration was willing to go to such lengths to destroy a few hundred militarily obsolete missiles is a testament to the profound shift in the perception of the MANPADS threat.

'we're on it'

Comparing US MANPADS efforts to the recommendations made by the RAND Corporation, Congressman Mica proudly observed in January 2005 that '[f]or the first time in many years that I've been around Congress, we're actually ahead of the report ... We're on it'.[30] They certainly were. Since the Mombasa attack in November 2002, the US has helped negotiate four international agreements on MANPADS control, tripled the amount of money it spends on critical small arms stockpile management and destruction programs, launched a multi-million dollar program to evaluate technical counter-measures for airliners and improved airport perimeter security. These efforts signal an unprecedented national about-face – from leading proliferator in the 1980s to anti-proliferation champion less than twenty years later. Other countries' efforts are also impressive. The regional leadership of Russia is noteworthy, as are the changes it has made to its own policies and practices. Israel, Australia and dozens of other countries have also pursued, or contributed to, critical policies and programs.

Only time will tell if these efforts are enough. The ubiquity, lethality and portability of MANPADS make them a daunting international security challenge – made significantly worse by short-sighted foreign policies and lax export and stockpile controls. Atoning for the proliferation sins of previous generations will take many years of diligent effort and millions, perhaps billions, of dollars in scarce government resources. Whether the international community can muster and sustain the resolve to see these efforts through remains to be seen.

future challenges of proliferation

Hot lead can be almost as effective coming from a linotype as from a firearm.

John O'Hara

If war were only about killing people and destroying things more efficiently, its history and future could be summarized in lists, charts and tables of ever-increasing ranges, ever more efficient and ever-lighter weapons and ever-higher numbers of dead and wounded. However, wars have contexts and those contexts affect when, where, how long and for what weapons will or will not be used. They also affect what happens to the weapons – both large and small caliber – after the fighting ends and combatants demobilize, disarm and re-integrate into society. All too often, their weapons are also reintegrated, only to re-surface in criminal violence and inevitable tensions.

Should a country be drawn into a long war, experience will probably force a number of innovations and modifications to existing government weapons and to those that come into the hands of non-state groups and private individuals. This diffusion matters when the weapons end up in the hands of criminals, terrorists or abusive national governments and their proxies.

Like diamonds, small arms are forever – at least some of them seem to be. The .30 caliber Krag rifle, which the US Army used for only eleven years, was retired in the early 1900s – to re-emerge in both world wars issued to military security guards. The M1911 .45 caliber pistol, which replaced an underpowered .38 caliber side arm in 1911 is another classic. It remained the Army's official side-arm until 1985, when the M9 Beretta 9 mm was adopted, bringing the US in line with other NATO armies. When, in the 1991 Gulf War, the fine sand of the Persian Gulf jammed the Berettas, troops broke out their old .45 pistols which, fortunately, had been stored and not destroyed. This 'no-confidence' vote by ordinary soldiers was ratified five years later in May 1996, when Heckler and Koch delivered a new 12-round Mk23 .45 to US Special Forces.

Another context of war in the twentieth century was the development of a permanent military-industrial complex whose overriding objective is developing and selling better – better at killing – weapons. Arms merchants, legal and illegal, are interested in profits; the fate of the old weapons is not their concern. With conventional Cold War arms control efforts focused on constraining nuclear technology and heavy conventional weapons, small arms transfers were unregulated and largely unmonitored by the USSR, the US and their allies. Something which is still being played out is the shift away from inter-state to intra-state wars and wars involving non-state actors. Other than skirmishes between India and Pakistan over Kashmir, the Eritrea-Ethiopian border war and the US-led invasions of Afghanistan and Iraq, most armed conflicts in the twenty-first century have been internal and ethnic, clan-based or tribal contests fought for political control, land or resources. These conflicts recycle themselves by recycling small arms as succeeding generations come of age.

If an ounce of prevention is better than a pound of cure, where are the opportunities for gaining control over the tons of weapons and ammunition that governments neither want nor need but also can't control or safeguard? Perhaps, even more important, are there small arms and light weapons in development that, in the hands of rebels, terrorists or other criminals, will pose a significant new threat? In this epilogue, I shall try to assess these threats and examine possible control strategies.

the future of small arms development

On July 1, 2002, *Jane's International Defence Review* carried an analytical essay: *Infantry weapons: the way ahead.* The author – an astute, long-time observer of doctrine, tactics, training and weapons – made three points. First, the infantry weapons currently in use by armies, insurgents and terrorists are the technology of 1945, with minor evolutions. Second, nothing currently being developed promises a truly revolutionary change equivalent to the impact of the machine-gun at the end of the nineteenth century. Third, the complexity of future weaponry will increase costs so much that complete replacement of weapons might well be considered too expensive, relative to other military requirements.

In a sense, the article was good news for those concerned about the proliferation and misuse of small arms, suggesting that their sophistication would not grow to an extent that might increase dangerous proliferation. Moreover, if equal numbers of new weapons did not replace old, this would lower the numbers in insecure storage facilities and susceptible to theft. Nonetheless, development will not stop and weapons in storage will remain a potential threat until they are destroyed.

the twin nemeses: size and weight

"The best things come in small packages" is a familiar saying. Criminals and terrorists would applaud this sentiment: in their worlds an undetected weapon gives attackers material and psychological advantages. Small weapons complicate the task of devising and implementing counter-measures; thousands of security guards and scanning machines are needed in office buildings, airports, ports, tunnels and other sensitive locations.

Of course, 'good guys' have uses for compact, lightweight weapons too. Ask soldiers in a military transport plane or traveling cross-country whether they want a full-size rifle or a compact one and most will opt for the latter, both because it's easier to get into position and allows the soldier to carry more ammunition or other supplies. Among the best known compact rifles are the AK-47 variants (the AK-102, -104, and -105), the Israeli Mini-Uzi and Micro-Galil (the latter modeled on the AK-47), and the Belgian F2000 and Chinese Type 95.

There is, however, a right and a wrong way to achieve compactness. The obvious solution, cutting the barrel, the longest and heaviest part of the weapon, is the wrong one, for short barrels lower the speed of the bullet. Back in the days of Prohibition, the bullet velocity of the mob's iconic weapon – the short barrel sub-machine-gun – was so anemic that even the body armor of the day could stop the bullets.

The preferred method is what could be termed 'compact commonality'. Compactness comes through compressing and shortening other parts and keeping the barrel longer. Commonality comes from keeping the same ammunition, inter-changeable parts, rate of fire and reliability; keeping training simple and the user confident. This also improves mobility and maneuverability. Of course, the features that commend a weapon to the military also make it attractive to illegal arms brokers, criminals, terrorists and others outside the law.

new uses, new threats from old weapons

Old weapons, like the proverbial Old Soldiers, never die. They simply fade into the background until the next war.

When wars end, controlling, accounting, removing and disposing of weapons is a major challenge. Satellite photographs can be used to count tanks on a military base but assault rifles, machine-guns, light mortars and MANPADS have to be counted by hand.

Weapons stockpiles can build up when countries re-equip their forces with new armaments. Rather than destroying the old weapons, they try to sell them. If they cannot find a buyer, they store them 'just in case'. Moreover, some weapons can be upgraded by fitting a new warhead or new tracking capability (for example replacing a radar guidance system with a laser one). The downside to improved capability is that countries under embargo, abusive governments, terrorists and insurgents who already have the old system or launcher need only to beg, borrow, steal or buy the new warhead or tracker to possess a more destructive weapon.

improvised explosive devices

Events in Iraq and Afghanistan starkly illustrate why destruction of excess weapons is the key to reducing conflict. More coalition troops have died or been seriously wounded by improvised explosive devices (IEDs) – than by any other weapon used by the insurgents.

Some may question why IEDs are included in a survey of small arms and light weapons, since explosives do not form part of the internationally accepted UN definition of small arms. However, looking at how IEDs can be used – shells opened, explosive extracted and repacked for a suicide bomb, buried along roads, placed in dead animals or put into abandoned vehicles – shows how easily they can be transported and how they do not need sophisticated support; characteristics they have in common with light weapons. Moreover, some of the munitions used in IEDs fall into the category of light weapons – for example, mortar rounds under 100 mm and rocket propelled grenades.

The source of these and other munitions used by Iraqi insurgents is well known: the three million tons of ammunition scattered around the country in insecure depots. The depots contain a smorgasbord of weapons, shells, shoulder-fired air defense munitions, rockets, mortar shells, rocket-propelled grenades and millions of rounds of ammunition. The good news is that coalition troops are destroying these depots: the bad news is that – even at the current, frenetic pace of 25,000 tons a month – the short-term impact will be minimal, because of the size of the stockpile.

This means the number of IED attacks is unlikely to decrease soon, particularly since new caches continue to be uncovered. The data from the Pentagon is not encouraging; in 2004 the number of IED attacks recorded against coalition and Iraqi security forces and civilians was 5,607 while in 2005 there were 10,593. IEDs will continue to be a deadly tool for insurgents as long as insecure stockpiles remain.

thermobarics

In Afghanistan and Iraq, one of the most potent weapons of the insurgents is anything but high technology – the rocket-propelled grenade (RPG), which came into service in Soviet and Warsaw Pact armies in the 1960s. Like the AK family, one variant, the RPG-7, has come to represent all models. Like the AK, the RPG-7 is extremely popular; it is in the arsenals of forty countries and an unknown number of insurgent groups. Rugged in design, with a re-usable launcher and an effective range of 670 m, RPGs cannot be jammed, because they do not rely on homing radar or heat-seeking. With a price tag ranging from twenty bottles of vodka in Chechnya, $150 on the European black market (in 2000) to $50 in Afghanistan (in 2004), RPGs are an inexpensive and effective weapon that can disable armored vehicles and even bring down helicopters. The ability to destroy helicopters in flight is not new. In Vietnam, ten per cent of helicopter losses were attributed to RPGs. Today's Apache attack helicopters and Blackhawk troop carriers are better armored and have components the Vietnam-era UH-1 Huey Utility helicopters did not have. Nonetheless, they can be brought down, as can the venerable and vulnerable Chinook transport helicopter still used by the US Army and Special Forces operating in Afghanistan and Iraq.

RPG-7s are getting technology makeovers. In 2004, China announced it was ready to sell a new, 'thermobaric' warhead for the RPG-7. Unlike the traditional high explosive round, this does not rely on shrapnel. Instead, the warhead sprays a fine, flammable, mist which then ignites, creating a fireball that burns into any openings, such as a cave entrance, doors or windows and around corners. Those who survive the fireball are asphyxiated, as the burning uses all the oxygen in the area. The US is designing its own line of man-portable thermobaric weapons. Its army already has thermobaric warheads for an automatic grenade launcher and shoulder-fired anti-bunker rocket launcher: ultimately, the Army wants a reliable thermobaric warhead for its new infantry weapon. This weapon will give soldiers – or terrorists – a capability that, in the US military, previously existed only in bombs carried by Air Force F-15E jet fighters.

grenades

A third old system showing new life is the lowly grenade. Classic war movies depict soldiers either lobbing grenades as far as possible into machine-gun nests or creeping up to an enemy foxhole in the dead of night and rolling in a grenade. All that will be lost if, in keeping with the general trend of removing the fighter from direct contact with the enemy, militaries perfect a self-guiding projectile for the 40 mm grenade launcher. The United States is studying the SCORPION (Self Correcting Projectile for Infantry Operations), which will follow a pre-computed, constantly updated, course from launcher to target, making corrections by firing bursts of air through micro-jets. If successful, the Pentagon believes this will be a longer-range (from 150 to 250 meters) and more precise weapon for combat in urban environments.

metal storm: a new light weapon

The history of weaponry is the contest between offense and defense: the new countered by the newer countered by the newest. In the early twentieth century, the tank was the infantry's answer to the machine-gun. A century later, the gun may restore the balance, with what some call the infantry's *Perfect Storm*.

The technology, and the Australian company that created it, is known as *Metal Storm*. The idea is simple: a curtain of projectiles guarantees hitting the target. This is an old concept: anti-aircraft gunners of World War II used it when they 'led' raiding enemy fighters and bombers. The US Navy's ship defense system, *Phalanx* – essentially a super-fast Gatling gun, designed to knock down sea-skimming anti-ship cruise missiles or to keep sea-borne terrorists and suicide bombers from getting too close (as happened to the USS Cole in the harbor of Aden, Yemen in October 2000) – is the radar-controlled successor to the anti-aircraft gun. However, physics limits even the multi-barreled Gatling gun to about 6,000 rounds per minute. The effect, while impressive, is hardly a curtain of lead.

Imagine now, instead of a belt or magazine-fed weapon, a number of pre-loaded, quick-loading barrels and a gun with no mechanical parts: no trigger, no hammer, no breech-block and (because the ammunition has no casing) no ejector mechanism. The only things that move are the bullets, hurtling down the barrel at pre-set speeds of between 600 and 1,000,000 rounds per minute. The high rate is possible because the bullets are loaded head to toe with a thin propellant film in between which, ignited by an electric current, fires the bullets. High pressure from the bullet moving down the barrel distorts the next bullet's shape so it fills the bore, blocking – momentarily – the electric current. When the fired bullet leaves the barrel, the pressure drops and the next bullet regains its shape and is fired. Whereas conventional machine-gun bullets emerge from the barrel thirty meters apart, Metal Storm prototypes have fired 180 rounds of 9 mm ammunition in .01 seconds: just ten centimeters apart.

In experiments, pods of pre-loaded tubes have successfully rapidly fired 20 mm and 40 mm grenades to between 300 and 2,200 meters. When linked to intruder detection devices, Metal Storm can replace anti-personnel minefields, for example around military bases. Because each tube is independent, there is no minimum number that must be linked. This allows for flexibility, both in the shape of the tube and the number of rounds. The company even has developed a pistol based on the same technology and in January 2006 was awarded a Pentagon research contract to develop a less-than-lethal configuration for uses such as controlling rioting.

getting control

In today's world, unsavory governments and non-state groups can acquire and apply rudimentary technology which, incorporated into 'improved' weapons, poses a real challenge to global small arms control. 'Dumb' munitions suddenly become 'smart' when combined with otherwise innocuous electronics and lasers. This is not new. What seems new is the ability of terrorists, criminals, renegade soldiers and guerrillas to cause many casualties and create extensive chaos and political upheaval in a very short time.[1] Graves throughout Africa: in Liberia, Sierra Leone, Côte d'Ivoire, Democratic Republic of Congo, Sudan, Eritrea and Ethiopia are mute testament to the deadly effects of recycled small arms and light weapons when governments fail to control their flow.

Iraq and Afghanistan ought to serve as warnings of what can happen in a failed, or failing, state where large numbers of weapons are wielded by abusive governments, criminals, insurgents, terrorists and private citizens. For all their military might, after more than fifty-three months in Afghanistan and thirty-six in Iraq, the coalition allies still find themselves trapped and steadily bled by a relatively small number of determined, ruthless, and to a certain degree innovative, fighters.

Countries in the developing world are not the only ones where large numbers die from small arms and light weapons. Sometimes, countries that first supplied weapons to the developing world suffer 'blowback', as did the USSR in the 1980s and now the US in Afghanistan. The G8 countries account for eighty-four per cent of the world legal arms trade, of which, in 2002, small arms were estimated to be worth approximately $4 billion. Belatedly, the G8 has acknowledged its responsibility by including conventional arms proliferation in the agenda of its annual meetings. At its gathering in 2003, the G8 singled out Africa as an area of special concern, promising aid to governments trying to curb the illegal arms trade. In a separate but related move, the European Union has thrown its support behind a proposed international arms trade treaty to regulate production and transfer of small arms and encourage destruction of stocks accumulated during the Cold War.

However, as so often happens when trying to control illegal use of legal commodities, progress is rarely uninterrupted. Many observers had expected the 2005 G8 meeting to endorse the EU's position on an arms trade treaty but it produced a very tepid, non-committal statement on what was 'discussed' and 'elaborated'; concluding with agreement that 'developing a common under-standing of governments' responsibilities would be an important step in tackling the undesirable proliferation of conventional arms' and that there was a 'need for further work to build a con-sensus for action'. Inconclusive as they may be, such efforts com-plement the eleven-year focus of the United Nations on the human and material devastation caused by the global trade in small arms and light weapons. In 2001, the UN held a landmark conference, from which came the *Programme of Action to Prevent, Combat and Eradicate the Illicit Trade in Small Arms and Light Weapons in All Its Aspects*. The *Programme*, a voluntary set of recommendations and guidelines for member states, reflected the disagreements that hamper effective control of conventional arms. What is needed are comprehensive programs that control supply, destroy stockpiles, curb misuse and reduce demand by removing or mitigating the abuses that undercut both personal and national development. One priority – alongside safeguarding and destroying existing stockpiles – should be pre-venting their accumulation in countries which currently do not have them.

The causes impelling those who engage in criminal, terror or abusive practices seem so innumerable as to defy solutions. While greater accountability can limit the magnitude of prolifera-tion, it will never stop the steady trickle of weapons that flows from one conflict to another. Even to approach that idyllic state, humanity will have to win the battle for 'hearts and minds', for universal human dignity and human rights – one person at a time.

sources

'Reaching for the Big Picture', in *Small Arms Survey 2005*. (Oxford University Press, 2005).

Iraq Survey Group *Final Report, Volume III, Section 6* (September 2004).

SIPRI, *2005 Yearbook, Armaments, Disarmament, and International Security*. (Stockholm International Peace Research Institute 2005).

articles

'The G8: Global Arms Exporters', *Control Arms Campaign*, June 22, 2005.

'Mini-M16s: a new class of small arms.' *Jane's International Defence Review*, December 2000 (unattributed).

C. J. Chivers, 'Ill-Secured Soviet Arms Depots Tempting Rebels And Terrorists', *The New York Times*, July 16, 2005.

Ned Colt, 'Iraq seen as 'one big weapons dump', NBC News, January 21, 2004.

Charles Q. Cutshaw, 'Infantry weapons: the way ahead', *Jane's International Defence Review*, Vol 35, January 2001.

Dan Drolette, 'Taking Ballistics by Storm', *Scientific American*, April 18, 1999.

Dan Drolette, 'Metal Storm multibarrel pod system progresses', *Jane's International Defence Review*, February 1, 2004.

Sandra Erwin, 'Army Rushes to Deploy Defensive Gear on Aircraft', *National Defense Magazine*, March 2004.

Joshua Kucera, 'US Army aims to create guided grenade', *Jane's Defence Weekly*, August 17, 2005.

Jonathan Marcus, 'Analysis: How thermobaric bombs work', *BBC News*, March 4, 2002.

Renae Merle, 'Low Tech Grenades a Danger to Helicopters', *Washington Post*, November 18, 2003.

Mike O'Dwyer, 'The War on Terrorism: Metal Storm – An Urban Warfare Weapon', Presentation at the *13th Annual SO/LIC Symposium and Exhibition*, Arlington, VA, February 2002.

Michael Renner, 'Arms Control Orphans', *Bulletin of Atomic Scientists*, January–February 1999.

Nicholas Rufford, 'Prime Suspect: Who Masterminded the Rocket Attack on MO6 Headquarters?', *Sunday Times*, September 24, 2000.

Noah Shachtman, 'When a Gun is More Than a Gun', *Wired Magazine*, March 20, 2003.

Jason Sherman, 'DOD Eyes New Approach To Avoid Iraqi Roadside Bombs', *InsideDefense.com*, February 23, 2006.

Eric Schmitt, 'Pentagon Widens Program To Foil Bombings In Iraq', *The New York Times*, February 6, 2006.

Brooks Tigner, 'EU Builds Strategy Against Small Arms', *Defense News*, October 24, 2005

Adam Ward, ed., 'Small arms and light weapons: Sharpening policy.' *IISS Strategic Comments*, Vol.11, Issue 4, June 2005.

Jim Wilson, 'Weapons of the Insurgents', *Popular Mechanics*, March 16, 2004.

glossary

AK-47   Russian assault rifle developed by Mikhail Kalashnikov. Between seventy and 100 million AK series weapons have been produced and these weapons are in the national inventories of fifty-eight countries and have been used in at least ninety conflicts worldwide.

Arms Broker   'any private individual or company that acts as an intermediary between a supplier and a recipient of weapons to facilitate an arms transaction in return for a fee'. (Source: Bondi, Loretta and Elise Keppler, 'Casting the Net: The Implications of the US Law on Brokering'.)

Black Market Transfer   arms deals which occur 'in clear violation of national and/or international laws and without official government consent or control; these transfers may involve corrupt government officials acting on their own for personal gain'. (Source: Small Arms Survey 2001.)

Conventional weapons   Weapons and military equipment, including aircraft, tanks and artillery that use non-nuclear explosives or kinetic energy to damage targets (Source: Nuclear Threat Initiative).

Diversion   The process by which small arms move from legal government control into the illicit realm. This can be authorized or unauthorized, intentional or unintentional. (Source: Small Arms Survey 2002.)

Grey market transfer arms transfers that involve governments, their agents or individuals acting to, 'exploit loopholes or circumvent national and/or international laws or policy'. (Source: Small Arms Survey 2001.)

Illicit transfer an arms transfer that violates international or national laws.

Inter-Service Intelligence (ISI) Pakistani intelligence agency that co-ordinated the intake and distribution of US-funded weapons and materiel for the Afghan rebels during the Soviet Occupation.

Irish Republican Army (IRA) Terrorist group formed in 1969 to unify Ireland and expel British forces from Northern Ireland. It is the armed wing of the legal political group Sinn Fein (Source: US State Department, *Patterns of Global Terrorism 1998*).

Kinetic energy weapon a device that relies on its speed, the hardness of its material (tungsten, for example), and its speed at impact to destroy a target by transferring its energy of momentum. Contrasting destruction modes are explosives and directed energy.

Legal transfer an arms transfer that conforms to international law, as well as the national laws of the importing and exporting states.

Less lethal weapons (LLW) devices explicitly designed and primarily employed to incapacitate or otherwise prevent individuals from engaging in destructive behavior while minimizing fatalities, permanent injury or damage to property and the environment. Also referred to as non-lethal weapons.

Man-portable Air Defense Systems (MANPADS) 'surface-to-air missile systems designed to be man-portable and carried and fired by a single individual and other surface-to-air missile systems designed to be operated and fired by more than one individual acting as a crew and portable by several individuals'.

(Source: United Nations Register of Conventional Arms 2004 Information Book).

Metal Storm   a potentially revolutionary electronic method of firing bullets or other projectiles so rapidly (theoretically at a rate of one million rounds per minute) that they constitute a virtual 'curtain of steel'.

Mujahedeen   Afghan guerrillas from the major ethnic groups who united to expel the Soviet military from Afghanistan and overthrow the Soviet-back Afghan government. Literally 'Holy Warrior' or 'Soldier of God'.

Programme of Action (PoA)   The outcome document from the July 2001 United Nations *Conference on the Trade of Small Arms and Light Weapons in All its Aspects*. The PoA has ten pillars of action on the national, regional and global levels to address small arms proliferation and misuse. The PoA is a politically binding (as opposed to legally binding) document, meaning its fulfillment is voluntary.

Small Arms and Light Weapons   A sub-category of conventional arms that can be operated and carried by one person or a small crew. The United Nations classifies small arms as revolvers and self-loading pistols, rifles and carbines, assault rifles, sub-machine-guns and light machine-guns. Light weapons are classified as heavy machine-guns, hand-held under-barrel and mounted grenade launchers, portable anti-tank and anti-aircraft guns, recoilless rifles, portable launchers of anti-tank and anti-aircraft missile systems and mortars of less than 100mm caliber. (Source: United Nations, Report of the Panel of Governmental Experts on Small Arms, 1997.)

Stinger (FIM-92) missile   US man-portable air-defense system first produced in 1979 and fielded in 1981. The infra-red-seeking, fire-and-forget anti-aircraft system was used by Afghan guerrillas to shoot down dozens of Soviet Aircraft during the 1980s.

Wassenaar Arrangement (WA)   an international institution that promotes transparency and information sharing regarding the transfer of conventional arms and dual-use items. The first multilateral agreement on MANPADS export controls was negotiated through the WA.

Weapons modularity the concept in designing weapons that views the component 'systems' in a 'system of systems' as inter-changeable sub-assemblies which, when combined on a common 'platform' produce a weapon with lethal and less lethal capabilities appropriate for an anticipated confrontation.

White market transfer also known as legal transfers, these transfers 'occur with either the active or passive involvement of governments or their authorized agents and in accordance with both national and international law'. (Source: Small Arms Survey 2001.)

websites

About.com   inventors.about.com

Air Force Historical Research Agency   www.au.af.mil

Anti-defamation League   www.adl.org

Arquebus   www.arquebus.com

BBC News   news.bbc.co.uk

Bonn International Centre for Conversion   www.bicc.de

Brady Center to Prevent Gun Violence   www.gunlawsuits.org

B'Tselem (The Israeli Centre for Human Rights in the Occupied Territories)   www.btselem.org

Canadian Medical Association Journal   www.cmaj.ca

Center for Defense Information   www.cdi.org

Centre for Humanitarian Dialogue   www.hdcentre.org

Columbia International Affairs Online   www.ciaonet.org

Conservation Force   conservationforce.org

Civil War Preservation Trust   www.civilwar.org

DEBKA*file*   www.debka.com

Douglas Farah   www.douglasfarah.com

Federation of American Scientists   www.fas.org/main

FirearmsID.com   www.firearmsid.com

Friends Committee on National Legislation   www.fcnl.com

The Fund for Peace   www.fundforpeace.org

Global Policy Forum   www.globalpolicy.org

Global Security Group   www.globalsecurity.org

Graphic Ghana   www.graphicghana.info

John Guilmartin   www.angelfire.com/ga4/guilmartin.com/index.html

Human Rights Watch   www.hrw.org

Institute for Security Studies   www.iss.co.za

Internal Displacement Monitoring Centre
   www.internal-displacement.org

International Action Network on Small Arms   www.iansa.org

International Physicians for the Prevention of Nuclear War
   www.ippnw.org

Iraq Coalition Casualty Count   www.icasualties.org/oif

Jane's International Defence Review   www.janes.com

Metal Storm Ltd   www.metalstorm.com

Al Mezan Center for Human Rights   www.mezan.org

Nairobi Secretariat on Small Arms and Light Weapons
   www.nbisecsalw.org

National Defense Magazine   www.nationaldefensemagazine.org

NBC News   www.msnbc.msn.com

Peace Magazine   www.peacemagazine.org

PBS   www.pbs.org

Popular Mechanics   www.popularmechanics.com

Quaker United Nations Office   www.quno.org

RAND Corporation   www.rand.org

Raytheon   www.raytheon.com

Redstone Arsenal   www.redstone.army.mil

Research Press   www.researchpress.co.uk

Ryerson University Research Services   www.research.ryerson.ca

Scientific American   www.sciam.com

Small Arms Survey   www.smallarmssurvey.org

South African Police Service   www.saps.gov.za

The Tribune of India   www.tribuneindia.com

United Nations   www.un.org

United States Department of Defense   www.defenselink.mil

United States Department of State   www.state.gov

Viva Rio   www.vivario.org.br

Wikipedia   en.wikipedia.org

Wired Magazine   www.wired.com

World Health Organization   www.who.int

notes

introduction

1.   Ken Silverstein, 'Comrades in arms: meet the former Soviet mobsters who sell terrorists their guns', *Washington Monthly*, January 1, 2000.
2.   Graduate Institute of International Studies, *Small Arms Survey 2004: Rights at Risk* (Oxford: Oxford University Press, 2004), pp. 163–164.
3.   Bruce Hoffman, *Inside Terrorism* (New York: Columbia University Press, 1998).
4.   Alex Schmid and Albert J. Youngman, *Political Terrorism: A New Guide To Actors, Authors, Concepts, Data Bases, Theories, And Literature* (Transaction Publishers, April 1998). See also Michael Stohl 'Demystifying Terrorism: The Myths and Realities of Contemporary Political Terrorism', in Michael Stohl (ed.) *The Politics of Terrorism* (Marcel Dekker, January 1988), pp. 1–28.
5.   Hoffman, *Inside Terrorism*, p. 42.

prologue

1.   Coincidentally, the Mississippi regiment had been commanded by Colonel Jefferson Davis. In fact, Davis' personal wartime experience with a 'real' rifle probably pre-disposed him to accept the recommendation of the Ordnance Board.

See Wikipedia, *http://en.wikipedia.org/wiki/rifle*, and Byron Farwell, 'Mississippi Rifle', in *The Encyclopedia of Nineteenth Century Land Warfare: An Illustrated World View* (W.W. Norton and Co., 2002), p. 565.

chapter one

1. Maharaj K. Koul, 'Kalashnikov: A weapon of choice', *The Tribune* (India), November 15, 1998, *http://www.tribuneindia. com/1998/98nov15/sunday/head7.htm*.

2. United Nations, Report of the Panel of Governmental Experts on Small Arms, A/52/298, *http://www.un.org/Depts/ddar/ Firstcom/SGreport52/a52298.html*.

3. Nick Paton Walsh, 'I sleep soundly', *The Guardian Unlimited*, October 10, 2003 *http://www.guardian.co.uk/g2/story/0.3604, 1059879,00.html*.

4. Robert Fisk, 'Dealer's Choice', *The Independent*, April 22, 2001, pp. 10–14.

5. Chris McNab, *The AK-47* (St. Paul: MBI Publishing, 2001), pp. 15–16; Duncan Long, *AK-47: The Complete Kalashnikov Family of Assault Rifles* (Boulder: Paladin Press, 1988), pp. 9–10; Val Shilin and Charlie Cutshaw, *Legends and Reality of the AK: A Behind-the-Scenes Look at the History, Design, and Impact of the Kalashnikov Family of Weapons* (Boulder: Paladin Press, 2000), pp. 19–21.

6. Terry Gander, *Guerrilla Warfare Weapons: The Modern Underground Fighter's Armory* (New York: Sterling Publishing Co., 1990), p. 52; Shilin and Cutshaw, *Legends and Reality of the AK*, pp. 19–21; Long, *AK-47*, pp. 9–10.

7. Walsh, 'I sleep soundly'.

8. Gander, *Guerrilla Warfare Weapons*, p. 53; Long, *AK-47*, p. 13; David Miller, *Illustrated Directory of 20th Century Guns* (London: Salamander Books Ltd., 2001), pp. 262–263.

9. Ministry of Defense of the USSR, *The Official Soviet AKM Manual: Operating instructions for the 7.62 mm Modernized Kalashnikov Rifle (AKM and AKMS)*, translated and with original illustrations by Maj. James F. Gebhardt, US Army (retired) (Boulder: Paladin Press, 1999); Shilin and Cutshaw, *Legends and Reality of the AK*, p. 37; Gander, *Guerrilla Warfare Weapons*, p. 56.

10. Fisk, 'Dealer's Choice'; Tom Parfitt, 'Kalashnikov gives name to 'manly' but less lethal products', *The Scotsman*, February 19, 2003, p. 15.

11. Larry Kahaner, *AK-47: The Weapon that Changed the Face of War* (John Wiley & Sons, Inc., 2006).

12. McNab, *The AK-47*, pp. 54–57; Kahaner, *The AK-47*, Chapter 3.

13. Author correspondence with A.A. Zavarzin, October 20, 2005. According to the Director of Foreign Economic Activity Department for Izhmash, the company that produces the AK-47, up until the 1980s the Soviet Union supplied AK-47 factories and rights to manufacture the AK-47 to twelve countries. Other countries also produced AKs without obtaining licenses. However, those rights and licenses have expired and Izhmash believes no countries or companies currently have any rights to produce AKs or use the AK brand.; Kahaner, *The AK-47*, Chapter 2; McNab, *The AK-47*, pp. 54–57; Shilin and Cutshaw, *Legends and Reality of the AK*, p. 34.

14. Walsh, 'I sleep soundly'.

15. Worldwide, there are between one and ten million Uzis and approximately seven million M-16s in circulation. Rachel Stohl and William Hartung, 'Hired guns', *Foreign Policy*, May/June 2004, pp. 28–29; Abdel Fatau Musah and Robert Castle, 'Eastern Europe's arsenal on the loose: Managing light weapons flows to conflict zones', *BASIC Occasional Paper 26*, May 1998.

16. Michael Wines, 'Symbols are important. So what does a gun symbolize?', *The New York Times*, October 7, 2005, p. A4.

17. Anti-Defamation League, 'International Terrorist Symbols Database', 2006, *http://www.adl.org/terrorism/symbols/default. asp*; Fisk, 'Dealer's Choice'.

18. Sami Faltas and Wolf-Christian Paes, 'Exchanging guns for tools: The TAE approach to practical disarmament—An assessment of the TAE project in Mozambique', *Bonn International Centre for Conversion Brief 29*, April 2004, p. 7, *http://www.bicc.de/publications/briefs/brief29/brief29.pdf*; Parfitt, ''Manly' But Less Lethal Products'.

19. Fisk, 'Dealer's Choice'.

20. Kahaner, *The AK-47*, Preface; Walsh, 'I sleep soundly'.

21. McNab, *The AK-47*, p. 63; Kahaner, *The AK-47*, Chapter 2.

22. John Walcott and David Rogers, 'Ship used to send arms to Contras said to aid delivery of East-Bloc arms to US', *Wall*

Street Journal, February 13, 1987, p. 1; William Godnick, Robert Muggah, and Camilla Waszink, 'Stray bullets: The Impact of Small Arms Misuse in Central America', *Small Arms Survey Occasional Paper 5*, October 2002, p. 5, *http://hei.unige.ch/sas/OPs/ OP05CentralAmerica.pdf*; George Gedda, 'Contras obtain 10,000 Polish AK-47s rifles, US Officials Say', *Associated Press*, August 31, 1985.

23. Kahaner, *The AK-47*, Chapter 5; Frank Smyth, 'Mysterious influx of Soviet and Chinese arms for Salvador rebels', *The Sacramento Bee*, June 4, 1989.

24. Gedda, 'Contras Obtain 10,000 Polish AK-47s'; United States Court of Appeals for the District of Columbia Circuit, *Final Report of the Independent Counsel For Iran Contra Matters*, 1993, Chapter 2, *http://www.fas.org/irp/offdocs/walsh*.

25. Godnick, Muggah, and Waszink, 'Stray bullets', p. 6.

26. Godnick, Muggah, and Waszink, 'Stray bullets', pp. 11 and 26; 'Firearms Deaths Decline', *Canadian Medical Association Journal*, 169, (10), 2003, *http://www.cmaj.ca/cgi/content/full/169/10/1064-a*.

chapter two

1. Koul, 'Kalashnikov'.

2. Fisk, 'Dealer's Choice'.

3. Graduate Institute of International Studies (Geneva), *Small Arms Survey 2002: Counting the Human Cost* (London: Oxford University Press, 2002), p. 104.

4. R.T. Naylor, 'The structure and operation of the modern arms black market', in *Lethal Commerce: The Global Trade in Small arms and Light Weapons*, eds. Jeffrey Boutwell, Michael T. Klare, and Laura W. Reed (Cambridge: American Academy of Arts and Sciences, 1995), p. 48; Graduate Institute of International Studies (Geneva), *Small Arms Survey 2003: Development Denied* (London: Oxford University Press, 2003), p. 13; *Small Arms Survey 2002*, pp. 66, 109, and 111, Box 3.1.

5. Graduate Institute of International Studies (Geneva), *Small Arms Survey 2001: Profiling the Problem* (London: Oxford University Press, 2001), pp. 141 and 190.

6. Adapted from Rachel Stohl, 'The tangled web of illicit arms trafficking', in *Terror in the Shadows: Trafficking in Money, Weapons, and People*, eds. Gayle Smith and Peter Ogden (Center for American Progress, October 2004), pp. 21–26. For specific information on the UN reports on Angola and Liberia see UN documents S/2000/203 and S/2001/1015.

7. Ruchita Beri, 'Coping with small arms threat in South Africa', *Strategic Analysis*, 24 (1), April 2000, *http://www.ciaonet.org/olj/sa/sa_apr00ber02.html*; Graduate Institute of International Studies (Geneva), *Small Arms Survey 2004: Rights at Risk* (London: Oxford University Press, 2004), p. 64.

8. Chris McNab, *The AK-47*, pp. 54–57; Jeffrey Boutwell, 'Weaponization of the Israeli-Palestinian peace process', *Brown Journal of International Affairs*, 9 (1), Spring 2002, p. 300.

9. *Small Arms Survey 2004*, p. 61; Marianne W. Zawitz, 'Guns used in crime', Bureau of Justice Statistics, July 1995, *http://www.firearmsid.com/Feature%20Articles/0900GUIC/Guns%20Used%20in%20Crime.htm*; Beri, 'Coping with small arms threat in South Africa'; South African Police Service, *Annual Report, 2004–2005* (South African Police Service, 2005), *http://www.saps.gov.za/saps_profile/strategic_framework/annual_report/index.htm*.

10. Wendy Cukier and Antoine Chapdelaine, 'Small arms, explosives, and incendiaries', in *Terrorism and Public Health: A Balanced Approach to Strengthening Systems and Protecting People*, eds. B. Levy and V. Sidel (Oxford University Press, 2002), pp. 155–174; Lora Lumpe, 'The US arms both sides of Mexico's drug war', *Covert Action Quarterly*, 61, Summer 1997, pp. 39–46, *http://www.fas.org/asmp/library/articles/us-mexico.htm*.

11. Small Arms Survey 2003, pp. 26–36.

12. Small Arms Working Group, 'Fact sheet: Small arms and natural resources', *http://fas.org/asmp/campaigns/smallarms/sawg.htm*; Kahaner, *The AK-47*, Chapter 5.

13. Matthew Brunwasser, 'Victor Anatoliyevich Bout – The embargo buster: Fueling bloody civil wars' (FRONTLINE/World, May 2002), *http://www.pbs.org/frontlineworld/stories/sierraleone/bout.html*.

14. Douglas Farah, 'Islamic fundamentalism, terrorism, and al Qaeda in Africa', remarks delivered at The American

Enterprise Institute, April 13, 2004, *http://www.aei.org/events/ eventID.786/ event_detail.asp*; Michael Isikoff, 'Iraq: Government deal with a merchant of death', *Newsweek*, December 20, 2004, p. 8.

15. Loretta Bondi and Elise Keppler, 'Casting the net: The implications of the US law on brokering' (The Fund for Peace, January 8, 2001), p. 8.

16. Naylor, 'The structure and operation of the modern arms black market', p. 48.

17. Brian Wood and Johan Peleman, 'Making the deal and moving the goods – The role of brokers and shippers', in *Running Guns: The Global Black Market in Small Arms*, ed. Lora Lumpe (London: Zed Books, 2000), p. 131.

18. Global Witness, 'The usual suspects: How the Liberian government supports arms trafficking and mercenary activities in West Africa', March 2003, *http://www.globalwitness.org/ reports/show.php/en.00026.html*, pp. 20–21.

19. Kathi Austin, 'Weapons in the Great Lakes region of Africa', in *Light Weapons and Civil Conflict*, eds. J. Boutwell and M. Klare (Rowman and Littlefield Publishers, Inc., 1999), pp. 36–39; Gregory Kipling, 'Old guns for a new war: The resurgence of arms smuggling in Costa Rica', *Peace Magazine*, July–September 2002, p. 6, *http://www.peacemagazine.org/archive/ v18n3p06.htm*; 'TV broadcasts intercepted rebel conversation', Caracol TV, Bogota, Colombia, August 28, 2000.

20. William Kistner, 'Sarkis Soghanalian: The cold war's largest arms merchant' (FRONTLINE/World, March 2001), *http://www.pbs.org/frontlineworld/stories/sierraleone/ soghanalian.html*.

21. Ken Silverstein, 'Comrades in arms', *The Washington Monthly*, 34 (1/2), January/February 2002, p. 21; Kistner, 'Sarkis Soghanalian'.

22. Douglas Farah and Kathi Austin, 'Victor Bout and the pentagon: Air America', *The New Republic*, January 23, 2006, pp. 11–13.

23. Owen Greene, 'Promoting effective global action on small arms: Emerging agendas for the 2006 review conference', Biting the Bullet Discussion Paper (International Alert/Saferworld/ University of Bradford, July 2005), *http://www.saferworld. org.uk/images/pubdocs/BtB%20Emerging%20issues.pdf*.

chapter three

1.   Kate Connolly, 'Kalashnikov: "I wish I'd made a lawnmower"', *The Guardian*, July 30, 2002, p. 2.

2.   Fisk, 'Dealer's Choice'.

3.   Wendy Cukier and Antoine Chapdelaine, 'Small arms: A major public health hazard', *Medicine and Global Survival*, Vol. 7, No. 1, April 2001, pp. 26–32.

4.   'Kabul prepares to disarm gun-loving people', *Reuters*, December 27, 2001; 'UN for end to Afghan gun culture', *Frontier Post* (Pakistan), January 9, 2002.

5.   'Internal displacement: Global overview of trends and developments in 2005', ed. Jens-Hagen Eschenbächer (Internal Displacement Monitoring Centre, March 2006), *http://www.reliefweb.int/library/documents/2006/idmc-gen-22mar.pdf*; Kahaner, *The AK-47*, Chapter 4.

6.   Mustafa Mirzeler and Crawford Young, 'Pastoral politics in the northeast periphery in Uganda: AK-47 as change agent', *The Journal of Modern Africa Studies*, 38, 3, 2000, p. 419.

7.   Eric Berman and Robert Muggah, 'Humanitarianism under threat: The humanitarian impacts of small arms and light weapons' (Small Arms Survey, March 2001), p. 8.

8.   Cate Buchanan and Robert Muggah, 'No relief: Surveying the effects of gun violence on humanitarian and development personnel' (Centre for Humanitarian Dialogue and SAS, June 2005), *http://www.hdcentre.org/datastore/Small%20arms/Norelief/No%20Relief_Eng2.pdf*.

9.   Anne Scott Tyson, 'Tough calls in child soldier encounters', *Christian Science Monitor*, June 27, 2002, p. 3.

10.   Kahaner, *The AK-47*, Chapter 3.

11.   Chris Smith, 'Light weapons and ethnic conflict in South Asia', in *Lethal Commerce: the Global Trade in Small Arms and Light Weapons*, eds. Jeffrey Boutwell, Michael T. Klare and Laura W. Reed (Cambridge, MA: American Academy of Arts and Sciences, 1995), p. 64; Peter Chalk, 'Light arms trading in SE Asia', *Jane's Intelligence Review*, March 1, 2001, *http://www.rand.org/commentary/030101JIR.html*; Kahaner, *The AK-47*, Chapter 3.

12.   Steve Coll, *Ghost Wars: The Secret History of the CIA, Afghanistan, and Bin Laden, From the Soviet Invasion to*

September 10, 2001 (Penguin Press, 2004), p. 221; Kahaner, *The AK-47*, Chapter 3; Pyotr G. Litavrin, 'Sources of small arms and light weapons procurement in Southwest Asia', in *Small Arms Control: Old Weapons, New Issues*, ed. UNIDIR (Geneva: UNIDIR, 1999), p. 232.

13.   John J. Lumpkin, 'Bin Laden's terrorist training combines math, missiles', *Associated Press*, October 9, 2001; Steve Coll, 'Anatomy of a victory: CIA's covert Afghan war', *Washington Post*, July 19, 1992, p. A1.

14.   Muhammad Shahedul Anam Khan, 'Linkages between arms trafficking and the drug trade in South Asia', in *Small Arms Control: Old Weapons, New Issues*, ed. UNIDIR (Geneva: UNIDIR, 1999), pp. 246–7.

15.   B'Tselm B'Tselem, 'Intifada Fatalities' (B'Tselem, 2006), *http://www.btselem.org/English/Statistics/Casualties.asp*; Samir Zaqout, Tahani Abdel-Rahman and Hussein Hamm, 'Case study: Northern Gaza strip small arms and community security perceptions: North Gaza' (Al Mezan Center for Human Rights, 2004), *http://www.mezan.org/document/small_wheapon_research_en.pdf*.

16.   Margot Dudkevitch, 'Tunnels keep Gaza terrorists awash in arms', *Jerusalem Post*, May 16, 2004, p. 3; and 'Palestinians smuggle weapons from Egypt into Gaza drastically bringing down prices', *Associated Press*, September 14, 2005; 'Palestinian terrorists pour tens of millions into a new arms stockpile', DEBKA *file* Exclusive Report, September 17, 2005, *http://www.debka.com/article_print.php?aid=1084*.

17.   Josef Federman, 'Palestinians enforce ban on weapons displays, in step toward ending lawlessness', *Associated Press*, September 30, 2005.

18.   Human Rights Watch, 'Small arms and human rights: The need for global action', in *Human Rights Watch Briefing Paper for the UN Biennial Meeting on Small Arms*, July 2003, p. 5.

19.   Riyadh Lafta, Les Roberts, Richard Garfield and Gilbert Burnham, 'The role of small arms during the 2003–2004 conflict in Iraq', *Small Arms Survey Working Paper 1*, September 2005, p. 11; Haider al-Moosawi, 'Pre-election gun boom in Baghdad', *Institute for War and Peace Reporting*, January 27, 2005, *http://iwpr.gn.apc.org/?s=f&o=245149&apc_state=heniicr2005*.

20. Lafta, et. al., 'The role of small arms during the 2003–2004 conflict in Iraq', p. 5, *http://icasualties.org/oif/default.aspx*; Charles Levinson, 'Cautiously, Iraqis open for business', *Christian Science Monitor*, January 4, 2006, p. 6.

21. Sameer N. Yacoub, 'Few Iraqis turning weapons over to US', *Associated Press*, June 2, 2003; Richard Atwood, 'Weapons of mass diffusion', *Mother Jones*, July 17, 2003, *http://www.motherjones.com/news/update/2003/07/we_483_01.html*; US Central Command, News Release Number 03–66–44, June 12, 2003.

22. John Diamond, 'Small weapons prove the real threat in Iraq', *USA Today*, September 29, 2003, p. 1A; Bill Gertz, 'Iraq arms caches exceed 8,700; Hunt continues', *Washington Times*, May 13, 2004, p. A3; *Small Arms Survey 2004*, p. 48.

23. Rachel Stohl, 'Small arms continue to plague Iraq', *Defense Monitor, Center for Defense Information*, Volume XXXIII, Number 3 – May/June 2004, pp. 3–4.

24. 'Charles Taylor: Profile of the former Liberian president', BBC, *http://news.bbc.co.uk/1/hi/world/africa/2963086.stm*.

25. Jeffrey Boutwell and Michael T. Klare, 'A scourge of small arms', *Scientific American*, Vol. 282, No. 6, June 2000, pp. 48–53; Global Witness, 'The usual suspects: Liberia's weapons and mercenaries in Côte d'Ivoire and Sierra Leone', March 2003.

26. Global Witness, 'The Usual Suspects'; Report of the Panel of Experts pursuant to Security Council Resolution 1343 (2001), paragraph 19, concerning Liberia, *http://www.un.org/Docs/sc/committees/Liberia2/1015e.pdf*.

27. 'Charles Taylor: A wanted man', CNN, December 4, 2003; The Special Court for Sierra Leone, 'Prosecutor vs. Taylor', *http://www.sc-sl.org/Taylor.html*.

28. Human Rights Watch, 'Liberia at a crossroads: Human rights challenges for the new government', *Human Rights Watch Briefing Paper*, September 2005, p. 2; Human Rights Watch, 'Bringing justice: The special court for Sierra Leone – Accomplishments, shortcomings, and needed support', *Human Rights Watch Report*, Vol. 16, No. 8(A), September 2004, p. 1.

29. Peter Batchelor, 'Intra-state conflict, political violence and small arms proliferation in Africa', in *Society under Siege:*

Crime, Violence, and Illegal Weapons, ed. Virginia Gamba (Institute for Security Studies, 1997), p. 117, *http://www. iss.co.za/pubs/Books/SocietyUnderSiege1/Batchelor.pdf*; Kahaner, *The AK-47*, Chapter 4.

30. Matt Schroeder, 'Issue brief 3: The illicit arms trade' (Federation of American Scientists, September 2005), *http://fas.org/asmp/campaigns/smallarms/IssueBrief3Arms Trafficking.html.*

31. Gander, *Guerrilla Warfare Weapons*, pp. 20–21.

32. 'Colombia plane hijacker sentenced', BBC, November 12, 2005, *http://news.bbc.co.uk/2/hi/americas/4430632.stm.*

33. 'Terrorists get weapons from the underworld', *Matamat* (Bangladesh), September 8, 2003, *http://www.matamat.com/ fullstory.php?gd=19&cd=2003-09-09*; Brady Center to Prevent Gun Violence, 'Guns and Terror: How Terrorists Exploit Our Weak Gun Laws' (Brady Center to Prevent Gun Violence, 2001), p. 3; Congressional Research Service, 'Foreign terrorists and the availability of firearms and black powder in the United States' (Congressional Research Service, May 2003).

34. Brady Center, 'Guns and Terror'.

35. *Small Arms Survey 2001*, p. 217.

36. Monte Reel, 'Brazil gun ban weighs a national', *The Washington Post*, October 1, 2005, p. A1; IANSA, 'There are around 17 million guns in Brazil' (IANSA, 2005), *http://www.iansa.org/regions/samerica/brazil-referendum.htm*; Joanna Wright, 'Firearms and drugs fuel conflict in Brazil's favelas', *Jane's Intelligence Review*, November 2005, pp. 36–41.

37. *Small Arms Survey 2003*, p. 61; Dr. Neil Arya, Address to the United Nations Conference on the Illicit Trade in Small Arms and Light Weapons in All its Aspects, 2001, *http://www.ippnw.org/SmallArmsAryaUN.html*; Ted R. Miller and Mark A. Cohen, 'Costs of gunshot and cut/stab wounds in the United States, with some Canadian comparisons', *Accident Analysis and Prevention*, 29, 1997, pp. 329–341; 'Small Arms and Global Health', WHO Contribution to the UN Conference on Illicit Trade in Small Arms and Light Weapons, July 9–20, 2001, *http://whqlibdoc.who.int/hq/2001/WHO_NMH_VIP_01.1.pdf.*

chapter four

1. 'Kalashnikov criticizes US for Venezuela arms export statement', *Interfax*, February 12, 2005.

2. Boutros Boutros Ghali, 'Supplement To An Agenda For Peace: Position Paper Of The Secretary-General On The Occasion Of The Fiftieth Anniversary Of The United Nations', A/50/60 – S/1995/1, January 3, 1995, para. 60–65.

3. United Nations Development Programme, 'Guidelines for reporting on implementation of the United Nations Programme of action to prevent, combat and eradicate the illicit trade in small arms and light weapons', p. 4, *http://www.undp.org/ bcpr/smallarms/docs/PoA_package.pdf.*

4. *Implementing the Programme of Action 2003: Action by States and Civil Society* (Biting the Bullet and IANSA, 2003); *International Action on Small Arms 2005: Examining implementation of the UN Programme of Action* (Biting the Bullet and IANSA, 2005).

5. Ibid.

6. Matthew Schroeder, 'Small arms, terrorism, and the OAS firearms convention', *FAS Occasional Paper 1*, March 2004, p. 45.

7. *International Action on Small Arms 2005*, p. 37; *Annual Report on the Progress of the Implementation of the Nairobi Declaration* (Nairobi Secretariat on Small Arms and Light Weapons in the Great Lakes Region and the Horn of Africa, 2005), *http://www.nbisecsalw.org/pdf/Nairobi%20Secretariat.pdf.*

8. *Canadian country report on PoA implementation*, 2005, *http://disarmament.un.org/cab/nationalreports/2005/CanadaUN-Report-SALW-2005-Final-eng.pdf*; *International Action on Small Arms 2005*, pp. 68–70.

9. *International Action on Small Arms 2005*, pp. 162–171.

10. 'Juan Michel, 'To disarm, body and soul: Brazilian churches participate in national disarmament campaign', *Viva Rio*, May 18, 2005, *http://www.vivario.org.br/english*; 'Partners in Peace: NGO contributions to the implementation of the UN's POA on Small Arms', IANSA pamphlet, July 2003; Rebecca Peters, 'Message from the Director', IANSA, January 21, 2005.

11. *International Action on Small Arms 2005*, pp. 125–127.

12. 'WAANSA hands over draft convention on small arms and light weapons to ECOWAS secretariat', IANSA, October 6,

2005, http://www.iansa.org/regions/wafrica/waansa-draft-convention.htm; 'Draft convention on small arms', Graphic Ghana, October 10, 2005, http://www.graphicghana.info/article.asp?artid=8485.

13. Adapted from Rachel Stohl, 'Reality check: The dangers of small arms proliferation', Georgetown Journal of International Affairs, 6 (2), Summer/Fall 2005, pp. 71–77.

14. Greene, 'Promoting effective global action on small arms', p. 6.

15. Jeremy P. Carver et. al., 'Model convention on the registration of arms brokers and the suppression of unlicensed arms brokering' (The Fund for Peace, 2001), http://www.fundforpeace.org/publications/reports/model_convention.pdf.

16. 'The control arms campaign', IANSA, http://www.iansa.org/control_arms/index.htm.

17. For more information on potential policy initiatives see Stohl, 'The Tangled Web of Illicit Arms Trafficking'.

18. Office of the Spokesman for the Secretary General, 'Use of sanctions under chapter VII of the UN charter' (UN, January 2006), http://www.un.org/News/ossg/sanction.htm; Small Arms Survey 2004, p. 265.

19. Human Rights Watch, 'Ripe for reform: Stemming Slovakia's arms trade with human rights abusers', Human Rights Watch Report, Vol. 16, No. 2(D), February 2004, http://hrw.org/reports/2004/slovakia0204.

20. Taras Kuzio, 'Ukraine: Look into arms exports', The Christian Science Monitor, February 12, 2002, p. 9.

21. Ibid; 'Lugar, Obama urge destruction of conventional weapons stockpiles', Nunn-Lugar Report, August 2005, p. 5, http://lugar.senate.gov/reports/Nunn-Lugar_Report_ 2005.pdf.

22. Boutwell and Klare, 'A scourge of small arms'.

23. IRIN, 'Afghanistan: Last ex-combatant disarmed under DDR' (irinnews.org, July 26, 2005), http://www.irinnews.org/report.asp?ReportID=48029&SelectRegion=Asia&SelectCountry=AFGHANISTAN.

24. Small Arms Working Group, 'Fact sheet: Small arms collection, destruction, and stockpile protection', 2003, http://fas.org/asmp/campaigns/smallarms/sawg.htm.

25. Jurgen Brauer and Robert Muggah, 'Completing the circle: Building a theory of small arms demand', Contemporary Security Policy, Vol. 27, No. 1, April 2006, pp. 138–154.

26.   David Atwood, Anne-Kathrin Glatz and Robert Muggah, 'Demanding attention: Addressing the dynamics of small arms demand', QUNO and Small Arms Survey, January 2006, *http://www.quno.org/geneva/pdf/disarmament-peace/ demanding-attention-op18–200601-English.pdf.*

chapter five

1.   'Stinger Update', *Congressional Record*, March 31, 1987, pp. 7557–7559.

2.   'Rebel Group Looks to Purchase Anti-air Missiles', *La Prensa*, 12 November 2003; Javier Baena, 'Leftist Rebels Earn Much Less Through Drug Trafficking Than Initially Believed', *Associated Press*, January 31, 2005.

3.   'MANPADS: Big Issue, Big Problem?' *Small Arms Survey 2004: Rights At Risk* (Oxford: Oxford University Press, 2004).

4.   Interview with senior US defense intelligence official, October 24, 2005.

5.   Mary T. Cagle, *History of the Redeye System* (Historical Division, US Army Missile Command, Redstone Arsenal, May 23, 1974); Michal Fiszer, 'On Arrows and Needles: Russia's Strela and Igla Portable Killers', *Journal of Electronic Defense*, January 1, 2004.

6.   Unpublished data from the Stockholm International Peace Research Institute. See also Central Intelligence Agency, 'Imports of Military Equipment and Material by North Vietnam in 1974', *Interagency Intelligence Memorandum*, January 10, 1975; 'The Soviet 'Strela' System: A Man-portable SAM', *Intelligence Memorandum* (Directorate of Intelligence, Central Intelligence Agency, July 23, 1970).

7.   'No Stinger Missiles for Saudi Arabia', *Congressional Record*, April 11, 1986, p. 7021.

8.   Daniel Byman, *Deadly Connections: States that Sponsor Terrorism* (New York: Cambridge University Press, 2005), p. 290; Robert Kupperman and Darrell Trent, *Terrorism: Threat, Reality and Response* (Stanford, CA: Hoover Institution Press, 1979), pp. 28–31; Office of Intelligence and Threat Analysis, *Terrorist Tactics and Security Practices* (Bureau of Diplomatic Security, US Department of State, 1994). The 'mad

dog of the Middle East' may have been the most brazen and outspoken of the early state sponsors of terrorists but he was not alone. Georgetown University Professor Daniel Byman's extensive research into state sponsorship of terrorism led him to conclude that '[d]uring the 1970s and 1980s, almost every important terrorist group has some ties to at least one supportive government.' See Byman, *Deadly Connections*, p. 1.

9.   Giles Foden, 'Who Else Was Out to Get Amin?', *The Guardian*, September 21, 1996; Greenway, 'Israel Admits 5 Held Over a Year As Terrorist; Israel Holds 5 Terror Suspects Seized in Kenya; Secret Trial Set', *Washington Post*, March 31, 1977. While difficult to corroborate, the *Post's* claim that the missiles came from Uganda is entirely plausible. Amin had access to an estimated 100 SA-7 missiles that he purchased from the Soviets in 1975, and was actively supporting other Palestinian radicals, including the PLO, at the time of the attack. See Arye Oded, *Islam and Politics in Kenya* (London: Lynne Rienner Publishers, 2000).

10.   H.D.S Greenway, 'Israel Admits 5 Held Over a Year As Terrorists', *Washington Post*, March 31, 1977.

11.   Unclassified Memo, Department of State, October 26, 1973.

12.   'Lufthansa Cancels Algiers Flights After Hijack Threat', *Aviation Week & Space Technology*, November 14, 1977; Milton Bengamin, 'Lufthansa Combats Terrorist Threats', *Washington Post*, November 15, 1977.

13.   Henry A. Kissinger to Members of the Cabinet Committee to Combat Terrorism, ''Intermediate' Terrorism', Memorandum, Secretary of State, June 5, 1976; Robert H. Kupperman, *Facing Tomorrow's Terrorist Incident Today* (US Arms Control and Disarmament Agency, October 1977), p. i.

14.   The account of flight 825 was compiled from information in David B. Ottaway, 'Rhodesian Air Crash Survivors Slain', *Washington Post*, September 5, 1978; Ottaway, 'Nkomo Says His Forces Hit Plane', *Washington Post*, September 6, 1978; 'Findings on Viscount airliner crash', *BBC Summary of World Broadcasts*, January 5, 1979.

chapter six

1.   George Crile, *Charlie Wilson's War* (New York: Grove Press, 2003), p. 16.

2.   Pakistani official Mohammad Yousaf claims that the Hind caused relatively few military casualties but were particularly hated because they were frequently used against civilians. Mohammad Yousaf and Mark Adkin, *Afghanistan: The Bear Trap* (Havertown, PA: Casemate, 1992), p. 177.

3.   Bill Gunston, *An Illustrated Guide to Military Helicopters* (New York: Prentice Hall Press, 1986), p. 100; Yousaf, *Afghanistan: the Bear Trap*, p. 177.

4.   The *Mujahedeen* were not the only ones awed by the seemingly invincible gunship. Nine thousand miles away, a Nicaraguan rebel battling the Soviet-backed and Hind-armed Sandinista government voiced the same mixture of awe and exasperation: 'You can fire a million shells into it and nothing happens'. Shirley Christian, 'Nicaraguan Rebel puts Missiles at 20', *The New York Times*, December 13, 1985.

5.   Charlie Wilson's exploits are expertly documented in *Charlie Wilson's War* by George Crile (New York: Grove Press, 2003).

6.   Interview with former staff member of the House Armed Services Committee, July 11, 2005.

7.   Steve Coll, *Ghost Wars* (New York: Penguin Books, 2005), p. 51; Crile, *Charlie Wilson's War*, p. 124; Alan J. Kuperman, 'The Stinger Missile and US Intervention in Afghanistan', *Political Science Quarterly*, Vol. 114, No. 2, 1999, p. 221; Robert M. Gates, *From the Shadows: The Ultimate Insider's Story of Five Presidents and How they Won the Cold War* (New York: Touchstone, 1996), p. 252.

8.   Crile, *Charlie Wilson's War*, p. 219.

9.   Coll, *Ghost Wars*, pp. 66, 81 and 103; Kuperman, 'The Stinger Missile and US Intervention in Afghanistan', p. 228; Crile, *Charlie Wilson's War*, p. 159. Much of the data on the program is still classified and therefore a full accounting is nearly impossible.

10.   Yousaf, *Afghanistan: The Bear Trap*, p. 83; Milt Bearden and James Risen, *The Main Enemy* (New York: Ballantine Books, 2003), pp. 129 and 274.

11.   Yousaf, *Afghanistan: The Bear Trap*, pp. 107–108.

12.   Coll, *Ghost Wars*, p. 67; Yousaf, *Afghanistan: The Bear Trap*, pp. 104–105; Kuperman, 'The Stinger Missile and US Intervention in Afghanistan', p. 232.

13.   Yousaf, *Afghanistan: The Bear trap*, pp. 88, 171 and 178; Crile, *Charlie Wilson's War*, pp. 159–160.

14. Milton Bearden 'Graveyard of Empires', in Gideon Rose, *How Did This Happen?* (New York: PublicAffairs, 2001), p. 87; Sarah E. Mendelson, *Changing Course: Ideas, Politics, and the Soviet Withdrawal from Afghanistan* (Princeton, NJ: Princeton University Press, 1998), p. 68; Crile, *Charlie Wilson's War*, p. 404.

15. Kuperman, 'The Stinger Missile and US Intervention in Afghanistan', pp. 222–233. Kuperman cites senior officials from the Reagan Administration who reportedly told him that Zia had been requesting the Stingers for over a year, but that the CIA had failed to convey this request.

16. Bearden, *The Main Enemy*, p. 201; Yousaf, *Afghanistan: the Bear Trap*, p. 181.

17. Donald M. Rothberg, 'Nearly Half of Senate Trying to Stop Fighter Sale', *The Associated Press*, May 25, 1982; Mark Starr, 'A Weapons Reward for Hussein', *Newsweek*, April 18, 1983; Roger Matthews, 'Hussein rebuffs Reagan over policy in Israel', *Financial Times*, March 16, 1984; John Goshko, 'Reagan Abandons Plan to Sell Stinger Missiles', *Washington Post*, March 21, 1984.

18. Allyn Fisher, 'Shamir Fears US Missiles Granted to Saudis could Fall into Terrorist Hands', *Associated Press*, May 27, 1984.

19. Christopher Madison, 'Stinger Missile May Not be Ideal for Job, but Time was Right for US-Saudi Deal', *The National Journal*, June 16, 1984.

20. Brad Knickerbocker, 'Administration Defends Sale of Stingers', *Christian Science Monitor*, June 6, 1984.

21. David Ottaway and John Goshko, 'Missiles Requested for the Saudis; White House Cites Fear of Escalation in Iran-Iraq War', *Washington Post*, March 12, 1986.

22. Bernard Gwertzman, 'Big Missile Sale to Saudi Arabia Opposed by Key Congress Panels', *The New York Times*, April 24, 1986; Steven V. Roberts, 'Senate Rejects Saudi Arms Sale, 73–33', *The New York Times*, May 7, 1986.

23. James Gordon, 'Congress Rebuffs Reagan Bid to Sell Missiles to Saudis', *Aviation Week & Space Technology*, May 12, 1986.

24. 'S. 2286-Stingers and Security Controls', *Congressional Record*, April 11, 1986, p. 7261.

25.   Interview with former Defense Department official, July 2005.

26.   Yousaf, *Afghanistan: The Bear Trap*, p. 182.

27.   Coll, *Ghost Wars*, p. 151.

28.   Yousaf, *Afghanistan: The Bear Trap*, p. 176.

29.   Sara Fritz, 'Even Backers Question Rebels Getting Stingers', *Los Angeles Times*, September 1, 1986.

30.   'Postscript: Legacy of Afghanistan Haunts Both Cold War Superpowers', *CNN*, March 7, 1999; Bearden, *The Main Enemy*, p. 247; Kuperman, 'The Stinger Missile and US Intervention in Afghanistan', p. 248.

31.   United States Central Command, Afghan Fusion Cell, *Stinger: One Year of Combat*, October 26, 1986, p. 11. In one case, a Hind pilot preemptively bailed out of his aircraft after the helicopter flying next to his was hit by a Stinger; Kuperman, 'The Stinger Missile and US Intervention in Afghanistan', p. 248; Yousaf, *Afghanistan: The Bear Trap*, pp. 174 and 186; Crile, *Charlie Wilson's War*, p. 438.

32.   Secretary of State to US Mission to NATO, 'Meeting of NATO Experts on East and South Asia', September 1987; Kuperman, 'The Stinger Missile and US Intervention in Afghanistan', p. 246.

chapter seven

1.   Yousaf, *Afghanistan: The Bear Trap*, p. 187.

2.   Yousaf, *Afghanistan: The Bear Trap*, p. 187; Lionel Barber, 'Iran Threatens to Use Stingers', *Financial Times*, October 12, 1987; Molly Moore and David B. Ottaway, 'Iran Said to Obtain US-Made Stingers; Afghan Rebels May Have Sold Missiles', *Washington Post*, October 10, 1987.

3.   Thomas Hunter, 'The Proliferation of MANPADS', *Jane's Intelligence Review*, September 1, 2001; 'Raytheon Electronic Systems low-altitude surface-to-air missile system family – FIM-92 Stinger', *Jane's Land-Based Air Defense*, January 8, 2004.

4.   Simon Saradzhyan, ''Stingers' May Mean Carpet Bombing', *Moscow Times*, October 9, 1999; John Cooley, 'Qaddafi linked to IRA arms shipment', *Christian Science Monitor*, November 9, 1987; 'Libya Denies Shipping Arms to IRA',

United Press International, November 6, 1987; 'The Libyan Connection', *The Economist*, March 31, 1990; Paul Quinn-Judge, 'Russia called fertile ground for nuclear proliferation', *Boston Globe*, July 3, 1994; Hunter, 'The Proliferation of MAN-PADS'.

5.   Robin Wright, 'US Bidding to Regain Missiles Sent to Afghans', *Los Angeles Times*, July 23, 1993.

6.   Robert C. Toth, 'Terror Use of Afghan Rebel Missiles Feared', *Los Angeles Times*, March 27, 1988.

7.   United Nations Security Council, *Report of the Panel of Experts on Somalia pursuant to Security Council resolution 1474 (2003)*, S/2003/1035, November 4, 2003. Some of the individuals interviewed by UN investigators claim that Aideed received forty-three or more missiles and that up to four of these missiles ended up in the hands of Somali arms merchants.

8.   Elaine Sciolino, 'US Shapes Plan to Get Missiles from Afghans', *The New York Times*, March 12, 1989.

9.   Uli Schmetzer, 'CIA Trying to Buy Back Missiles Given to Afghans', *Chicago Tribune*, December 6, 1992; Coll, *Ghost Wars*, pp. 11–13 and 337.

10.   Coll, *Ghost Wars*, p. 337.

11.   Schmetzer, 'CIA Trying to Buy Back Missiles Given to Afghans'; Coll, *Ghost Wars*, pp. 11–13 and 337. Most reports on the buyback program are anecdotal and impossible to corroborate. For example, in 1992, the Pakistani Secretary-General for Foreign Affairs claimed that '[r]ecently we helped buy back 100 Stinger missiles from the Afghans and gave them back to the US administration'. Since the US embassy refused to comment on the Pakistani's claim, and Pakistan provided no evidence to back it up, there is no way to know if it is accurate. Anwar Iqbal, 'Official: Pakistan Helped US Buy Back Missiles from Afghan Rebels', *United Press International*, December 13, 1992.

12.   Interview with former Defense Department official, July 2005. See 'Afghan Rebel Bars Return of US Stinger', *The New York Times*, March 14, 1989; Schmetzer, 'CIA Trying to Buy Back Missiles Given to Afghans', *Chicago Tribune*, December 6, 1992.

13.   See Yousaf, *Afghanistan: The Bear Trap*, p. 103; *Tackling Small Arms and Light Weapons: A Practical Guide for Collection and*

Destruction (Bonn International Center for Conversion and the Monterey Institute for International Studies, February 2000), p. 8.

14. Molly Moore, 'CIA Falters in Recovery of Missiles; Blunders Alleged in Plan to Buy Back Afghan Stingers', *The Washington Post*, March 7, 1994; Coll, *Ghost Wars*, p. 337.

15. Coll, *Ghost Wars*, p. 12.

16. John F. Burns, 'The Fiercely Faithful', *The New York Times*, February 14, 1996.

17. Steve Coll provides the first public summary of this meeting. See *Ghost Wars*, pp. 336–340.

18. 'Afghans Refuse to Return US Stinger Missiles', *Los Angeles Times*, August 20, 1993.

19. Moore, 'CIA Falters in Recovery of Missiles'; Kathy Gannon, 'Afghan Warlord Releases Nine Hostages Held for a Year', *Associated Press*, July 22, 1994.

20. General Accounting Office, *Handheld Missiles Are Vulnerable to Theft and Undetected Loss* (GAO/NSAID, September 1994), pp. 4 and 5.

21. Coll, *Ghost Wars*, p. 232.

22. Interview with Robert Sherman, September 2005. See also Robert Sherman, 'The Real Terrorist Missile Threat, and What Can be Done About It', *FAS Public Interest Report*, Autumn 2003.

23. Ibid.

24. Interview with Robert Sherman. See also Sherman, 'The Real Terrorist Missile Threat, and What Can be Done About It'; the *Congressional Record*, September 24, 1987, pp. 25098 – 25099.

25. For more information on the Gilday case, see Tom Seppy, '2 Arrested, Warrants Issued for 2 More in Alleged Arms-Export Conspiracy', *Associated Press*, November 25, 1986; Nancy Lewis, 'Plot to sell Military Equipment to Libya, Syria Is Alleged in Court Here', *The Washington Post*, November 26, 1986; Lewis, 'US Alleges Syria-Exporter Arms Ties; Businessmen's Talks at Embassy Said to have Centered on Weapons', *The Washington Post*, December 7, 1986.

26. David Hughes, 'US Uncovers Extensive Efforts to Procure Weapons for Iran', *Aviation Week & Space Technology*, February 1, 1988; 'US Customs Agents Arrest Iranian Father and Son', *PR Newswire*, January 15, 1988.

27. For more information on the Moley case, see Leonard Doyle, 'Irishmen Convicted of Plot to Buy Missile', *The Independent*, December 12, 1990; 'Three Convicted of Conspiring to Buy Missile for IRA', *The Associated Press*, December 11, 1990.

28. Assistant Secretary of Defense for Command, Control, Communications, and Intelligence, *Physical Security of Sensitive Conventional Arms, Ammunition, and Explosives* (US Department of Defense, August 12, 2000), *https://134.11.61.26/CD9/Publications/DoD/Man/Man%205100.76-M%2020000812.pdf*; General Accounting Office, *Handheld Missiles Are Vulnerable to Theft*, p. 27.

29. General Accounting Office, *Handheld Missiles Are Vulnerable to Theft*, p. 29.

30. Matthew Brunwasser, 'From Ukraine, a New Kind of Arms Trafficker', PBS.org, May 2002, *http://www.pbs.org/frontlineworld/stories/sierraleone/minin.html*.

31. Owen Bowcott, 'FBI Charges Six Over IRA Arms Deal', *The Guardian*, November 13, 1992.

32. USAF Manned Aircraft Combat Losses 1990–2002, Air Force Historical Research Agency, *http://www.au.af.mil/au/afhra/wwwroot/short_studies/USAFMannedAircraftCombatLosses1990_2002.pdf*; Michal Fiszer, 'On Arrows and Needles: Russia's Strela and Igla Portable Killers', *Journal of Electronic Defense*, January 1, 2004; Jim Anderson, 'War, Drought, Ineptitude, May Doom Millions in Sudan', *United Press International*, October 5, 1990.

33. Jon Swain, 'Riddle of the Rwandan assassin's trail', *Sunday Times*, April 4, 2004.

34. David Hughes, 'FAA Examining Missile Threat', *Aviation Week & Space Technology*, August 16, 1993; Interview with Herb Calhoun, May 11, 2005.

35. The National Transportation Safety Board concluded that a fuel-related explosion in the center wing fuel tank was the most likely cause of the crash. See 'Congress Prods Bush Administration to Curb Missile Threat', *Airport Security Report*, March 26, 2003.

36. The account of the December plenary is based on a June 2005 interview with Joe Smaldone.

37. These regimes are the Nuclear Suppliers Group, the Zangger Committee, the Missile Technology Control Regime, the

Australia Group, the Nuclear Nonproliferation Treaty, the Biological and Toxicological Weapons Convention, the Chemical Weapons Convention and (when applicable) START I.

chapter eight

1. Dora Tsavdaridis, 'Passengers Cheat Death on Flight 582', *The Daily Telegraph*, November 29, 2002; Christine Spolar, 'People Thought They Were Seeing Things', *Chicago Tribune*, November 29, 2002.

2. United Nations Security Council, *Report of the Panel of Experts on Somalia pursuant to Security Council resolution 1474 (2003)*, S/2003/1035, November 4, 2003; Marc Lacey, 'Investigation in Kenya: Missiles Fired At Israeli Plane Are Recovered', *The New York Times*, December 7, 2002.

3. 'Bill Requiring Missile Defense Protections for Airbus A380 Aircraft Introduced in Congress', *Federal News Service*, June 15, 2005.

4. See Philip Shenon, 'Missile Threat is Bringing Stricter Rules for Airports', *The New York Times*, March 20, 2003; Jeanne Meserve, 'US Eyes Overseas Airports for Missile Threats', *CNN*, August 7, 2003; Subcommittee on Aviation, *Hearing on the Transportation Security Administration's Perspective on Aviation Security*, October 16, 2003.

5. 'News Conference with Senator Barbara Boxer (D-CA); Senator Chuck Schumer (D-NY); Representative Steve Israel (D-NY); Representative John Mica (R-FL)', *Federal News Service*, April 2, 2003.

6. 'Israel Urges Curbs on Small Missile Sales After Kenya Plane Attack', *Agence France Presse*, December 12, 2002.

7. Much of the information on Russian MANPADS initiatives, policies and programs comes from a written correspondence from a Russian government official, April 19, 2005.

8. Interview with US government official, December 2005.

9. 'APEC moves to protect aircraft from terrorist missiles', *Agence France Presse*, November 13, 2005.

10. Government Accountability Office, *Further Improvements Needed in US Efforts to Counter Threats from Man-Portable Air Defense Systems*, May 2004.

11. William Keller, *Arm in Arm: the Political Economy of the Global Arms Trade* (New York: Basicbooks, 1995), p. 2 and International Institute for Strategic Studies, *The Military Balance 1998/99* (London: Oxford University Press, 1998), pp. 306–309.

12. Raymond Bonner and Ian Fisher, 'At Iraqi Depot, Missiles Galore and No Guards', *The New York Times,* October 17, 2003.

13. David Lamb, 'Iraq's Conventional Arms Supply Bigger than US Thought', *Los Angeles Times,* October 17, 2003.

14. Douglas Jehl and David Sanger, 'US Expands List of Lost Missiles', *The New York Times,* November 6, 2004.

15. 'Anti-Missile Technology: Calling the shots', *The Engineer,* September 24, 2004.

16. This number is derived from a combination of tangible costs, such as the value of destroyed aircraft, and costs of a more theoretical nature, namely the estimated losses to consumer and producer surpluses. James Chow et al., *Protecting Commercial Aviation Against the Shoulder-fired Missile Threat* (Santa Monica, CA: RAND Corporation, 2005).

17. Ibid, p. 17.

18. Sarah Chankin-Gould and Matthew Schroeder, 'ASMP Issue Brief #1: MANPADS Proliferation', January 2004, *http://fas.org/ asmp/campaigns/MANPADS/MANPADS.html.*

19. Correspondence with RAND Analyst Marvin Schaffer, November 7, 2005; Chow, *Protecting Commercial Aviation Against the Shoulder-fired Missile Threat,* pp. 23–29; 'Shield in the Sky', *Flight International,* August 30, 2005.

20. Interview with senior US defense intelligence official, October 24, 2005.

21. *Associated Press,* September 7, 1979; Ken Silverstein and Judy Pasternak, 'A Market in Missiles for Terror', *Los Angeles Times,* March 6 2003; Richard Reeves, 'The Palme Obsession; The Murder Sweden Can't Forget – Or Solve', *The New York Times,* March 1, 1987.

22. 'Vigilant Eagle Airport Protection System', Raytheon Company, *http://www.raytheon.com/products/vigilanteagle.*

23. An Irish Excess Ordnance Team reportedly finished the destruction job shortly afterward.

24. Interview with State Department official, May 2005.

25. *Report of the General Secretariat of the Organization of American States on the Diversion of Nicaraguan Arms to the United Self*

Defense Forces of Colombia, OEA/Ser.G, CP/doc. 3687/03, January 6, 2003.

26.   'Nicaragua: Bolanos folds on missile destruction plan', *Latin American Weekly Report*, November 16, 2004.

27.   'Nicaraguan Congress Blocks President from Destroying More Anti-aircraft Missiles', *Associated Press Worldstream*, February 16, 2005.

28.   Pablo Bachelet, 'Nicaragua to Reveal Details about Stockpiled Weapons', *The Miami Herald*, February 27, 2005; 'Rumsfeld Confident that Nicaragua is Keeping Missiles Secure', *States News Service*, October 14, 2005.

29.   Program costs provided by US government official, February 2006.

30.   Angela Kim, 'Congress 'On Top Of' MANPADS Issues, Rep. Mica Says', *Aviation Daily*, January 26, 2005.

epilogue

1.   C. J. Chivers, 'Ill-Secured Soviet Arms Depots Tempting Rebels And Terrorists', *The New York Times*, July 16, 2005, p. 1.

index